THE WISE WOMAN WRITES

Embracing Your Creative Voice

by

Vanessa McKay

Copyright © 2025 Vanessa McKay

All rights reserved. No part of this book may be reproduced, distributed or transmitted in any form or by any means, including photocopying, recording or other electronic or mechanical methods, without the prior written permission of the author, except in the case of brief quotations embodied in critical reviews and certain other non-commercial uses permitted by copyright law.

For permission requests, please contact the author at vanessamckay.com.

First Edition
ISBN: 978-1-7637824-4-0 (paperback)

Published in Australia by Tea Time Press

Discover the writer you were meant to become. Have you spent decades nurturing others' dreams while setting your own writing aspirations aside? The time for your creative renaissance has arrived.

The Wise Woman Writes celebrates the unique creative advantages that come with a half-century of living and invites you to harness the power of your life experience on the page. Drawing on cutting-edge neuroscience that confirms the creative advantages of the mature brain, this guide illuminates how women over fifty possess neural networks perfectly calibrated for nuanced storytelling and profound creative connections. Far from being past your prime, you're neurologically primed for your most authentic and powerful writing.

From transforming life transitions into compelling narratives to establishing a sustainable writing practice amid ongoing responsibilities, this book offers practical strategies tailored specifically for women navigating creativity in their wisdom years. You'll learn to excavate your authentic voice and create meaningful work that reflects your accumulated wisdom.

Written with compassion, insight and reverence for the unique creative journey of women in their second act, *The Wise Woman Writes* is both guide and companion for those ready to claim—or reclaim—their identity as writers.

Your most resonant stories don't lie in the past; they're waiting to be written now, with the depth and clarity that only your years of experience can provide. The page is calling. Your voice matters. It's time to answer.

INTRODUCTION

Stirring inside you is a creative restlessness that won't be quieted, a story that demands to be told, or simply the recognition that you have something valuable to say. Whatever brought you here, you're not alone. Every year, I have the privilege of working with women just like you who are ready to claim their voices and honour their creative calling.

You may have spent decades putting everyone else's needs first: your children, your partner, your parents, your employer. You may have convinced yourself that writing was a luxury you couldn't afford, a dream better left to younger people with more time and fewer responsibilities. You have been carrying stories for years, waiting for the right moment to begin.

Here is what I want you to know: that moment is now.

At fifty, sixty, seventy or beyond, you are not too late to the writing life; you are arriving precisely when you are meant to. Your brain is becoming more creative, not less. Your decades of experience have given you emotional depth and wisdom that younger writers are still developing. The challenges you have faced, the relationships you have navigated, the losses you've endured, and the joys you've celebrated—all of this is creative capital that no amount of formal education can replace.

This book emerged from my work with hundreds of women who discovered their writing voices in their wisdom years. I have watched teachers become memoirists, nurses become novelists, and mothers become poets. I have seen women transform decades of life experience into powerful prose that resonates with readers around the world. Most importantly, I have witnessed the profound personal transformation that happens when a woman finally gives herself permission to take her creative work seriously.

The chapters ahead will guide you through every aspect of developing a sustainable, fulfilling writing practice. We'll explore the unique advantages you bring to creative work at this life stage, help you excavate your authentic voice from beneath years of adaptation to others' expectations, and provide practical strategies for building a writing life that honours both your creative needs and your ongoing responsibilities.

You will discover how to transform your life experiences into compelling narratives, navigate the emotional complexities of writing about family and difficult experiences, and create work that connects your personal insights to universal themes. Whether you are drawn to memoir, fiction, poetry or essays, this book will help you develop the skills and confidence to express yourself powerfully on the page.

Before you turn to the first chapter, I want you to do something radical: give yourself permission to want this. Permission to believe that your stories matter. Permission to claim time and space for your creative work. Permission to call yourself a writer, even if you have never published a single word.

You have a lifetime of material to draw from and decades of creative work ahead of you. Your most important writing may still be waiting to be discovered. The page is calling, and it's time to answer.

Welcome to your writing life. Let us begin.

CONTENTS

Introduction

1. The Creative Renaissance — 1
2. Taking Stock — 9
3. Permission to Begin Again — 17
4. Excavating Your Authentic Voice — 25
5. From Caretaker to Creator — 35
6. The Comparison Trap — 47
7. Working with Memory — 59
8. Honouring Your Body's Wisdom — 75
9. Alchemising Loss and Grief — 91
10. Reimagining Your Story — 105
11. Writing the Wisdom Years — 121
12. Legacy on the Page — 135
13. Creating Sustainable Writing Rhythms — 151
14. Beyond Memoir — 167
15. Finding Your Creative Community — 183
16. The Ongoing JourneyAcknowledgements — 199

About the Author — 215

References — 216

THE CREATIVE RENAISSANCE

'I've been thinking about writing for years,
but somehow there was always something more pressing,
more important. Now, at fifty-three, I wake up with stories
demanding to be told. What changed?'

– Sarah

If you're reading this book, you have felt that pull—the sudden or gradual awakening of creative urgency that seems to arrive with the middle years. You are not imagining it, and you are certainly not alone. There is a perfect storm of factors that converge around age fifty that makes this the ideal time for women to embrace their writing voice.

The creative threshold women experience around fifty isn't just about having more time (though that's part of it). It's a convergence of psychological, neurological and social factors that create what researchers call 'optimal conditions for authentic self-expression' (Al-Khouja et al., 2022).
After decades of performing roles—daughter, student, employee, wife, mother—many women reach a point where they're less concerned with meeting others' expectations and more interested in exploring their own truths. This shift

from external validation to internal satisfaction is crucial for authentic creative work.

By fifty, you've lived through enough experiences to have stories worth telling and insights worth sharing. You've navigated relationships, career challenges, loss, joy, disappointment and triumph. This isn't just life experience—it's material that only you can write about from your unique perspective.

While it might sound morbid, the growing awareness of finite time becomes a creative catalyst. When 'someday' transforms into 'now or never', many women find the courage to pursue dreams they've deferred.

Why Now Is the Perfect Time to Write

- For women whose children are grown, there's often a sudden availability of mental and emotional bandwidth that's been occupied for decades. One client described it as 'finally having room in my brain for my own thoughts.' This isn't just about physical time—it's about the psychic space required for deep creative work.

- Many women in their fifties have either achieved what they set out to accomplish in their careers or recognise that the corporate ladder no longer holds appeal. This can initially feel disappointing, but it often becomes liberating. 'I spent 25 years climbing someone else's mountain,' one workshop participant told me. 'Now I want to plant my own flag.'

- Whether you're actively planning retirement or it's still years away, the fifties often mark the beginning of thinking about 'what's next'. Writing offers a bridge between the structured work life and the open canvas of later years. It's something you can begin now and carry forward indefinitely.

- There is something powerful that happens when women begin thinking about what they want to leave behind. The stories of your grandmother that were never written down, the family history that lives only in your memory, the lessons learned through hard experience—these begin to feel urgent in a way they never did in your thirties.

- By now, most women have developed what psychologists call 'learned mastery'—the confidence that comes from successfully navigating decades of challenges. You've raised children, managed crises, built careers, survived losses. Writing a story or finishing a memoir starts to feel achievable rather than impossible.

- This might be the most liberating factor of all: by now, many women have reached the point where they're willing to disappoint some people in service of being authentic. The people-pleasing that often keeps women from sharing their real thoughts begins to feel less important than telling their truth.

The Neuroscience of Creativity After Fifty

Here is where it gets interesting: your ageing brain is becoming more creative, not less. Recent neuroscience research reveals several factors that make the mature brain particularly suited for creative work.

As we age, our brains use both hemispheres more equally—a phenomenon called bilateral processing. While younger brains are more specialised (left brain for logic, right brain for creativity), mature brains integrate both sides more fluidly. This means you can access both analytical and intuitive thinking simultaneously, making for richer, more complex creative work.

The brain's inhibitory mechanisms—the ones that make you second-guess and self-censor—decrease with age. While this can sometimes mean saying things you shouldn't, it also means your creative ideas flow more freely. You're literally neurologically designed to care less about what others think of your creative output.

Your mature brain has decades of patterns stored in its neural networks. This 'crystallised intelligence' allows you to make connections and see patterns that younger writers might miss. Your metaphors are richer, your insights deeper, because you're drawing from a vast database of lived experience.

Neuroscientists have identified the default mode network—the brain's resting state that is active when we're not focused on a specific task. This network, which is crucial for creativity, becomes more active and more interconnected as we age. Those moments of daydreaming or mind-wandering that increase in midlife? They're not signs of cognitive decline—they're your brain's creative engine running in the background (Callard & Margulies, 2014).

Dopamine (the reward chemical) decreases overall with age; the brain becomes more selective about what triggers its release. This means you're naturally drawn towards activities that provide genuine satisfaction rather than just external rewards. If writing calls to you now, it's likely because your brain recognises it as truly rewarding work.

Contrary to popular belief about ageing and memory, certain types of memory improve with age. Semantic memory (facts and concepts) and procedural memory (skills and habits) remain strong or even improve. This means you can access the vast store of information and experiences you've accumulated while developing new skills like the craft of writing.

The hormonal changes of menopause, while challenging, also offer some surprising creative advantages: lower oestrogen levels are associated with decreased concern about social approval and increased willingness to speak truths that might be uncomfortable. This can translate into more authentic, bold writing. Anthropologist Margaret Mead coined the term *postmenopausal zest* to describe the energy and focus many women experience after menopause. Freed from the hormonal fluctuations of reproductive years, many women report clearer thinking and increased drive towards meaningful projects.

The Social Permission Shift

Society's expectations for women also shift in ways that support creative pursuits:

- While becoming 'invisible' as an older woman can be painful, it also offers freedom. When you're no longer being evaluated primarily on your appearance or availability to others, you can focus on what you want to create and express.
- Culture grants permission for older women to be truth-tellers, wisdom-keepers and story-sharers in ways that younger women aren't always allowed. This social permission can be powerfully liberating for authentic expression.

Common Concerns and Why They Don't Apply

- *It's too late to start:* numerous authors published their first books after 50, 60, even 70. Laura Ingalls Wilder published *Little House on the Prairie* at 65. Grandma Moses began painting at 78. Your timeline is your own.
- *I'm not tech-savvy enough:* writing itself hasn't changed; it's still about putting words on paper (or screen). The publishing landscape offers more

options than ever, many of them simpler than traditional routes.

- *No one cares about old women's stories:* the demographic of readers over 50 is one of the largest and most engaged reading audiences. Your peers want stories that reflect their experiences, and younger generations are hungry for the wisdom and perspective that comes with age.

When you combine the psychological freedom, the neurological advantages, the hormonal shifts and the social permission that come with this life stage, it creates what can only be described as optimal conditions for authentic creative expression. This isn't about settling for a 'hobby' in your golden years. This is about recognising that your brain, your experience and your circumstances have aligned to give you superpowers you didn't have at twenty-five or thirty-five. The stories that want to be told through you now are stories that could only be written by someone who has lived what you've lived, learned what you've learned, and reached the freedom that comes with this unique life stage.

The question isn't whether you're qualified to write—it's whether you're willing to honour what's trying to emerge through you.

Writing
Exercise

Take a moment to identify which of these factors resonates most strongly with you. Write for ten minutes about how this particular aspect of your life stage is calling you towards creative expression. This will become part of your personal manifesto for why now is your time to write.

TAKING STOCK

'At fifty-five, I finally understood that every heartbreak, every triumph, every mundane Tuesday was research for the stories I was meant to tell. My life wasn't the thing that got in the way of my writing—it was my writing.'

– Elena

You may think you need to travel to exotic places or live through extraordinary events to have something worth writing about. This couldn't be further from the truth. Right now, you possess something that no published author, no matter how successful, can replicate: your unique combination of experiences, perspectives and accumulated wisdom.

At this stage of life, you're not starting from scratch; you're sitting on a goldmine of creative capital that has been decades in the making. The challenge isn't finding something to write about; it's recognising the treasure you already possess and learning to mine it effectively.

Every experience you've lived through—the beautiful and the brutal, the momentous and the mundane—has contributed to your creative reservoir. Think of yourself as a master craftsperson who has spent decades collecting the finest materials. Your failed relationships taught you about resilience and the complexity of love. Your career frustrations revealed insights about ambition, compromise and authenticity. The way you raised children (or chose not to) gave you perspectives on nurturing, sacrifice, and the evolution of identity. Even your grocery shopping habits reflect your values, your relationship with abundance or scarcity and your connection to community.

The beauty of writing from accumulated life experience is that you don't have to make things up—you simply have to recognise the stories that are already there. Your divorce wasn't just a personal upheaval; it was a masterclass in reinvention. Your mother's illness wasn't just a time of caregiving; it was an education in grace under pressure. Your promotion at forty-eight wasn't just career advancement; it was proof that women can bloom at any age.

Consider how differently you see the world now compared to your younger self. At twenty-five, a friend's betrayal might have felt like the end of the world. At fifty-five, you understand the layers of hurt, insecurity and miscommunication that often underlie such actions. This depth of understanding, this emotional intelligence earned through experience, is what gives your writing its power.

Your perspective is irreplaceable because it's been shaped by factors no one else has experienced in quite the same combination. You came of age during specific historical moments, navigated unique family dynamics, made particular choices at crucial crossroads, and learned lessons that only your specific journey could teach.

This isn't about being special or extraordinary; it's about being authentically you. The way you see the world has been filtered through your particular lens of gender, generation, geography, socioeconomic background, education, relationships, and countless other factors. When you write from this authentic perspective, you offer readers something they literally cannot get anywhere else.

Think about the books that have impacted you most deeply. Often, they're not about exotic adventures or extraordinary people. They're about ordinary humans navigating universal experiences of love, loss, growth and failure told through one person's unique lens with such honesty and insight that they illuminate something universal.

Your unique perspective includes not just what you've experienced, but how you've processed and integrated those experiences. The questions you ask, the connections you make, the patterns you notice are the gifts of your particular way of seeing. A teacher sees the world differently than an entrepreneur. A mother of four has a different perspective than a woman who chose to remain childless. Someone who married their high school sweetheart brings different insights than someone who found love at fifty.

None of these perspectives is better or worse; they're simply different, and that difference is valuable. Your job as a writer isn't to be everyone; it's to be authentically yourself, trusting that your truth will resonate with others who need exactly the story you have to tell.

The Power of Writing from Accumulated Wisdom

Wisdom isn't just knowledge—it's knowledge that has been tested, refined and integrated through experience. You've learned not just what happened, but what it meant. You've had time to see how stories end, to understand the consequences of choices, to recognise patterns that were invisible when you were living them.

This accumulated wisdom gives your writing several distinct advantages:

- **Emotional distance:** you can write about difficult experiences without being overwhelmed by them. The divorce that devastated you at 35 can be explored with compassion and insight at 55, because you've had time to heal and understand.

- **Pattern recognition:** you can see themes in your life that weren't apparent while you were living them. The thread of resilience that runs through seemingly separate experiences. The way certain types of people or situations repeatedly showed up, offering lessons you needed to learn.

- **Contextual understanding:** you understand how personal experiences connect to larger cultural, generational and historical contexts. Your story of workplace discrimination isn't just personal—it reflects broader societal changes. Your experience of caring for ageing parents illuminates universal themes about mortality, duty and love.

- **Hard-won insights:** you've learned lessons that can only be gained through living. You know that some things that seem catastrophic at the time redirect us towards better paths. You understand that people are more complicated than heroes and villains. You've learned that healing is possible, that growth never stops, that it's never too late to change course.

- **Perspective on time:** you understand the weight of moments differently. You know which memories endure and which fade, which experiences shape us, and which merely pass through us. This gives your writing a different relationship with time and meaning.

Writing from accumulated wisdom doesn't mean writing from a place of having it all figured out. It means writing from a place of having wrestled with questions long enough to understand their complexity. It means offering not answers, but better questions. It means writing with the humility that comes from experience and the confidence that comes from having survived and thrived.

Your accumulated wisdom allows you to write with what Buddhist teacher Pema Chödrön calls 'tender heart' and 'fierce compassion'—the ability to look honestly at difficult truths while holding yourself and others with loving kindness. This combination of clarity and compassion is what makes writing from this stage of life so powerful.

Writing Exercise

1: Experience Mapping

Create three columns on a page:

Column 1: Experiences

List significant experiences from your life (both positive and challenging). Include:

- Major transitions (marriage, divorce, career changes, moves)
- Challenges overcome (illness, loss, financial struggles, relationship difficulties)
- Moments of joy or fulfilment (achievements, celebrations, connections)
- Everyday experiences that shaped you (how you were parented, your first job, a meaningful friendship).

Don't worry about order or importance—just let memories flow.

Column 2: Lessons/insights

For each experience, note what you learned or how it changed you. What insights did this experience provide? How did it shape your worldview?

Column 3: Universal themes

Identify the universal human themes each experience touches on (love, loss, courage, betrayal, hope, fear, growth, etc.).

2: Unique Perspective Identification

Complete these prompts:

- Because of where and when I grew up, I see the world as …

- Because of my role as [mother/daughter/professional/caregiver], I understand …

- Because I've experienced both _____ and _____, I know that …

- Something I see differently than most people my age is …

- A belief I held strongly when younger that I now question is …

- A truth I've learned that I wish I could tell my younger self is …

3: Wisdom Distillation

Choose one experience from your list and write a letter to someone who might be going through something similar.

Share what you wish you had known, what helped you, what you learned in the aftermath. Write as if you're sitting across from them at a kitchen table, sharing hard-won wisdom with love and honesty.

This isn't about being preachy or prescriptive; it's about sharing your truth in service of others who might need exactly the perspective you have to offer.

Reflection Questions:

- Which experiences surprised you by making it on to your list?
- What patterns do you notice across your experiences and insights?
- Which universal themes appear most frequently in your life story?
- What aspects of your unique perspective feel most valuable to share?

Remember: your life experiences aren't obstacles to overcome before you can write—they are the very foundation of your creative power. Every year you've lived, every challenge you've faced, every joy you've experienced has been preparing you for this moment when you finally trust yourself enough to tell your truth.

PERMISSION TO BEGIN AGAIN

> 'At fifty-seven, I felt like I was starting from scratch. Then I realised—I wasn't starting from nothing. I was starting from everything I've ever been, known, and learnt. That's not starting over. That's starting with abundance.'
>
> – Margaret

If you have picked up this book, chances are you've wrestled with that persistent inner voice that whispers, 'It's too late for you.' Perhaps you've watched younger writers achieve success and felt that familiar sting of missed opportunity. Maybe you've started writing projects only to abandon them when they didn't immediately match your vision of what good writing should look like. Let's talk about dismantling those barriers and discovering that beginning again at midlife isn't just possible; it is powerful.

The belief that creativity has an expiration date is one of our culture's most damaging myths, and women bear its weight disproportionately. We're conditioned to believe that artistic achievement belongs to the young, that talent must be discovered early, and that by fifty, our creative ship has sailed.

This narrative is false and runs the risk of robbing the world of some of its most profound voices.

Consider these late bloomers: Laura Ingalls Wilder published her first *Little House* book at sixty-four. Penelope Fitzgerald didn't publish her first novel until she was fifty-eight and went on to win the Booker Prize at eighty, Annie Proulx first published at fifty, Harriet Doerr was seventy-four when her first novel was published.

But here's what's even more significant than these famous examples: neuroscience research shows that our brains don't peak creatively in youth. Dr. Gene Cohen's (2019) groundbreaking work on creativity and ageing reveals that our brains continue developing new creative capacities throughout our lives. The neural pathways that connect our left and right brain hemispheres strengthen with age, allowing for more integrated, nuanced thinking, exactly what great writing requires.

Your five decades of living haven't disqualified you from writing; they've been preparing you for it. Every relationship you've navigated, every challenge you've overcome, every moment of joy or sorrow has been adding layers to your creative reservoir. The young writer writes from possibility; the wise woman writes from knowledge.

One of the greatest obstacles facing midlife writers is the weight of our own expectations. We've spent decades developing expertise in other areas: raising children, building careers, managing households, and we have internalised the belief that competence should come quickly. When our first attempts at writing don't match our vision, we assume we lack talent rather than recognising we lack practice.

This is where the perfectionist trap snares us. We want to write like the authors we admire, forgetting that they've been writing for decades, that their polished prose represents countless hours of revision, that their 'overnight success' was probably twenty years in the making. We compare our first drafts to their final manuscripts and find ourselves wanting.

But mastery isn't the goal; authentic expression is. Your job isn't to write like Toni Morrison or Elizabeth Strout (though you can certainly learn from them). Your job is to write like you with all your particular wisdom, humour, heartbreak and hope. The world doesn't need another perfect writer; it needs your specific way of seeing and saying.

This shift in perspective is liberating. Instead of asking, 'Is this good enough?' we can ask, 'Is this true to my experience?' Instead of 'Will this impress others?' we can ask, 'Does this capture what I meant to say?' The focus moves from external validation to internal authenticity, and that's where real writing happens.

There's a Zen concept called 'beginner's mind' that involves approaching something with openness, eagerness, and freedom from preconceptions. For the midlife writer, this doesn't mean pretending you haven't lived or learned. It means bringing curiosity to your craft while honouring the depth of your experience.

Beginner's mind allows you to be playful with language, to experiment without judgement, to try forms and genres without having to commit to being 'that kind of writer'. It gives you permission to write badly in service of eventually writing well. It reminds you that every published author was once exactly where you are now staring at a blank page, wondering if they had anything worth saying.

But you bring something to the page that the twenty-five-year-old writer cannot: perspective. You know that most problems that seem catastrophic work out somehow. You understand that relationships are complex, that people contain multitudes, that life is both harder and more beautiful than you once imagined. You've witnessed patterns across decades that allow you to see themes and connections that escape younger writers.

This combination of beginner's mind with experienced eyes is a unique creative advantage. You can approach the craft with curiosity while drawing from a deep well of lived experience. You can be gentle with yourself as a beginning writer while trusting the wisdom of your content. The key is remembering that beginning again is not the same as starting over. You're not erasing everything you've been; you're adding writing to the fullness of who you are.

Writing Exercise

This exercise will help you identify and release the beliefs that are keeping you from fully embracing your writing journey.

1: Identifying Your Creative Blocks

Complete the following sentences as quickly as possible, without editing:

- I would write every day if only …
- I can't start writing until …
- Real writers are …
- I'm too old to …
- I'm not qualified to write because …
- If I were serious about writing, I would …
- I would share my writing if …

2: Rewriting Your Story

Now, take each limiting belief you've identified and rewrite it as a permission statement:

- Instead of *I can't start writing until I have a perfect home office.*
  o Write: *I give myself permission to write anywhere—at the kitchen table, in the car, in a notebook on my lap.*

- Instead of *Real writers have degrees and awards.*
  o Write: *I give myself permission to be a real writer simply because I write.*

3: Your Creative Manifesto

Using your permission statements, write a brief manifesto for your writing life. Begin with: *I give myself permission to …* and let it flow. This is your personal creative constitution, your reminder of what you have decided is true about your writing journey.

Keep this manifesto somewhere you can see it regularly—taped to your computer, in your writing notebook, on your bathroom mirror. Read it whenever that old voice of limitation tries to derail your creative momentum.

4: The Wisdom Inventory

Make a list of all the ways your life experience has prepared you for writing:

- What difficult experiences have given you compassion?
- What relationships have taught you about human nature?
- What work have you done that gave you insight into how the world operates?
- What losses have deepened your understanding of what matters?
- What joys have you experienced that deserve to be shared?

This is not about turning your life into material (though you may choose to). It's about recognising that you don't come to writing empty-handed. You come rich with understanding, and that understanding will inform everything you write, whether fiction or nonfiction, poetry or prose.

Remember: beginning again isn't about discarding everything you've been; it is about adding writing to the magnificent accumulation of your becoming.

EXCAVATING YOUR AUTHENTIC VOICE

'For years, I wrote the way I thought I should write—the way my English teacher would approve, the way my mother would find acceptable, the way that wouldn't make waves. When I finally wrote from my gut, using words that felt like mine, I discovered I'd been whispering when I had something to roar.'

– Diana

Your authentic voice isn't something you need to create from scratch; it's something you need to uncover. After decades of adapting your communication style to different roles (mother, wife, employee, daughter, friend), your true voice may feel buried under layers of learned behaviour and external expectations. This chapter is about archaeological work: carefully excavating your genuine voice from beneath the accumulated sediment of other people's preferences, judgements and requirements.

Before we can write in our authentic voice, we need to recognise all the other voices that have taken up residence in our heads. These aren't necessarily negative influences; many have served important purposes in our lives but now they interfere with our authentic expression.

Think of voice influences as falling into several categories:

Authority voices: these come from teachers, bosses, parents, and other figures who held power over us. They often carry messages about proper writing, acceptable topics, and appropriate tone. You might hear echoes of your high school English teacher insisting you never start a sentence with 'And' or 'But' or a professor who made you feel your personal experiences weren't worthy of academic attention.

Cultural voices: these represent the broader social expectations about how women should communicate. They whisper that you shouldn't be too direct, too angry, too confident or too vulnerable. They suggest that certain topics are 'unladylike' or that your experiences aren't universal enough to matter. These voices carry decades of conditioning about feminine propriety and acceptability.

Professional voices: years in the workforce have likely shaped how you communicate. If you've spent decades in corporate environments, you might default to business-speak even in creative writing. If you've been in helping professions, you might struggle to centre your own story rather than focusing on others' needs.

Family voices: these are perhaps the most complex because they're wrapped up in love and loyalty. They might discourage you from writing about family secrets, from expressing anger or disappointment, or from presenting a version of events that differs from the family narrative. They can make you feel guilty for claiming your own perspective.

Inner critic voices: often a composite of all the above, these voices have internalised criticism and doubt. They question your right to take up space on the page, your qualifications to speak on various topics, and the value of your particular perspective.

The goal isn't to silence all these voices—some carry wisdom worth preserving—but to recognise them as influences rather than absolute authorities. When you can identify whose voice is speaking in your head, you can make conscious choices about whether to listen.

Distinguishing Between External Expectations and Internal Truth

One of the most challenging aspects of finding your authentic voice is learning to distinguish between what you genuinely think and feel versus what you've been conditioned to think and feel. Women are particularly susceptible to this confusion because we're socialised from birth to be attuned to others' needs and expectations, often at the expense of our own inner knowing.

External expectations manifest in writing as:

- Topic avoidance: steering clear of subjects you find compelling because they're inappropriate, too personal, or not important enough
- Tone policing: softening your natural directness, adding unnecessary qualifiers, or apologising for your opinions
- Perspective minimisation: describing your experiences as 'just' your story, as if your viewpoint is less valid than others'
- Content filtering: editing out the messy, complicated or contradictory parts of your experience to present a more palatable narrative.

Internal truth, by contrast, feels urgent and necessary. It's the thought that keeps returning, the story that demands to be told, the perspective that feels essential to share. It might make you uncomfortable—not because it's wrong, but because it's honest. Internal truth doesn't worry about being likeable or acceptable; it worries about being accurate to your experience.

Here's a practical way to test whether something comes from external expectation or internal truth: when you write it, do you feel energy or depletion? Authentic voice tends to energise, even when the content is difficult. Borrowed voice tends to drain, leaving you feeling like you're performing rather than expressing.

Internal truth also has a physical quality. You might feel it as warmth in your chest, a sense of rightness, or even a slight rebellious thrill. External expectations often feel heavier, accompanied by anxiety about judgement or consequences.

Finding the Courage to Write in Your Own Voice

Identifying your authentic voice is one thing; actually using it requires courage. By midlife, many women have spent decades prioritising others' comfort over their own truth-telling. The prospect of writing authentically can feel both thrilling and terrifying.

The fear is understandable. Your authentic voice might:

- Express anger that others find uncomfortable
- Share experiences that challenge others' narratives
- Reveal vulnerabilities that feel too raw to expose
- Take positions that not everyone will agree with
- Claim authority in areas where you feel like an imposter.

But consider what happens when you don't use your authentic voice: you write words that feel hollow, stories that leave out the most compelling parts, essays that dance around the point you most want to make. You might gain approval, but you lose the profound satisfaction of genuine expression.

Courage in writing doesn't mean being reckless or cruel. It means being honest within appropriate boundaries. You can write your truth without destroying others. You can express anger without attacking. You can share vulnerability without oversharing.

Start small. Choose one piece of writing—a journal entry, a letter, a short story—and commit to writing it in your most authentic voice. Notice what happens in your body as you write. Notice what wants to be said that you normally wouldn't say. Notice the relief that comes with finally expressing what you really think.

Remember that your authentic voice serves a purpose beyond personal satisfaction. In a world full of generic content and borrowed perspectives, your particular way of seeing and saying is a gift. The experiences that shaped you, the insights you've gained, the wisdom you've accumulated—these create a voice that only you can offer.

Your authentic voice isn't just about you; it's for all the women who need to hear that someone else has thought their forbidden thoughts, felt their complicated feelings, and found ways to articulate experiences that seemed unspeakable.

Writing
Exercise

This multi-part exercise will help you identify the various voices that influence your writing and begin to excavate your authentic voice from beneath them.

1: Voice Mapping

Create five columns on a piece of paper with these headers:
- Authority voices
- Cultural voices
- Professional voices
- Family voices
- Inner critic voices.

Under each column, write down specific messages you've internalised about writing, communication or self-expression. Be as specific as possible. Instead of just 'be nice,' write 'Mum always said if you can't say something nice, don't say anything at all' or 'Mrs Johnson marked down my paper because I used "I" too much.'

2: Voice Dialogue

Choose the three strongest voices from your mapping exercise. Write a dialogue between these voices and your authentic self about a topic you've been wanting to write about but have been holding back on.

For example:

Inner critic: *You can't write about your divorce. What will people think?*

Authentic self: *I have insights about rebuilding your life that could help other women.*

Family voice: *But it will hurt the kids to have their business out there.*

Authentic self: *I can write about my experience without exploiting theirs.*

Let this dialogue continue until you feel you've heard all sides, and your authentic voice has had a chance to respond to the concerns.

3: Truth Testing

Write about the same topic in three different voices:
1. The 'appropriate' version: write as if you're trying to please everyone—family, critics, society. Notice how this feels in your body.

2. The 'rebellious' version: write as if you're deliberately trying to shock or offend. This isn't your authentic voice either, but it can help you access suppressed thoughts.

3. The 'truth' version: write from your gut, saying what you actually think and feel, without trying to please or shock anyone.

Compare these three versions. Which felt most energising to write? Which feels most true to your actual experience?

4: Voice Affirmation

Complete these statements:

- My authentic voice wants to say …
- When I write in my true voice, I feel …
- The world needs to hear my perspective because …
- I give myself permission to write about …
- My voice matters because …

5: Authentic Voice Commitment

Choose one piece of writing you've been avoiding or sanitising. Commit to rewriting one paragraph, one page, or one section in your most authentic voice. Set a deadline for completing this—not for perfection, but for honesty.

Write yourself a letter of commitment:

'Dear [Your Name], I commit to writing about [topic] in my authentic voice by [date]. I understand this might feel scary, but I trust that my truth deserves to be expressed. I will be kind to myself if it's imperfect, and proud of myself for being genuine.'

6: Daily Voice Practice

For the next week, end each day by writing one paragraph about something that happened, using your most authentic voice. Don't worry about craft or polish—focus on honesty. Notice which days feel easier and which feel harder. Notice what topics bring out your most genuine expression.

Remember: your authentic voice isn't a performance or a persona—it's simply what happens when you tell the truth in your own words. It may take time to feel natural, but every moment you practise writing authentically, you're reclaiming a part of yourself that belongs entirely to you.

FROM CARETAKER TO CREATOR

> 'I spent thirty years putting everyone else's needs first—my children's, my husband's, my parents', my boss's. When I finally carved out two hours on Saturday mornings for writing, my daughter asked if I was having a midlife crisis. I said, "No, honey. I'm having a midlife awakening."'
>
> – Patricia

The transition from caretaker to creator is one of the most profound shifts a woman can make, and one of the most necessary. For decades, you've likely been the one who remembers everyone's appointments, manages the emotional temperature of the household, and puts others' needs before your own. This caretaking role, whether in families, workplaces or communities has been essential work, but it may have come at the cost of your own creative expression.

Making space for your writing life doesn't mean abandoning your caring nature or neglecting your responsibilities. It means finally including yourself in the circle of people you care for. It means recognising that your creative work has value not just for you, but for everyone whose life you touch.

A woman who honours her own creativity teaches others, especially other women, that creative expression is not selfish luxury but essential nourishment.

The fantasy of perfect creative conditions such as unlimited time, a picture-perfect dedicated writing space and no interruptions, can keep us from writing as surely as any external obstacle. Real creative work happens in the spaces between responsibilities, in moments carved from busy lives, in corners claimed from cluttered houses.

Reclaiming creative space starts with reframing what 'space' means. It's not just physical (though having a designated writing spot helps); it's also temporal, mental and emotional. Creative space is any environment where you can think your own thoughts, follow your own curiosities, and express your own truth.

Physical space: you don't need a perfect office. You need a space that signals to your brain that it's time to create. This might be a corner of your bedroom with a small desk, a spot at the kitchen table that becomes 'yours' during certain hours, or even a clipboard and notebook that travels with you. The key is consistency—training your mind to associate a particular place with creative work.

Some women find that the ritual of claiming space is as important as the space itself. Clearing the dining room table, lighting a candle, putting on noise-cancelling headphones, or simply moving to a different chair can create the psychological boundary between caretaking mode and creating mode.

Temporal space: this is where the biggest battles are fought. Finding time to write when you're managing multiple responsibilities requires both strategy and stubbornness. Start by tracking how you actually spend your time for a week. You might discover pockets of possibility you didn't know existed: the twenty minutes while dinner simmers, the hour before anyone else wakes up, the commute time that could be used for voice memos.

The key is starting smaller than feels worthwhile. Fifteen minutes of daily writing is more valuable than waiting for the perfect two-hour block that never comes. Those small increments add up, and they train your brain to shift into creative mode quickly.

Mental space: perhaps the most challenging space to claim is mental. Our minds are cluttered with ongoing mental to-do lists, worries about family members, and the constant low-level vigilance that comes with being responsible for others' well-being. Creating mental space for writing requires practice in setting down these mental burdens, even temporarily.

Some techniques that help:

- Brain dump: before writing, spend 5 minutes writing down everything you're worried about or need to remember. This clears mental space without forgetting important things.

- Transition rituals: develop a consistent routine that signals to your brain it's time to shift from caretaker to creator—making tea, reading a favourite poem, or taking 5 deep breaths.

- Permission slips: literally give yourself permission to focus on your writing for the next however many minutes, knowing you'll return to other responsibilities afterwards.

Caretaking often requires emotional availability, being attuned to others' feelings, managing family dynamics, providing support during difficult times. Creative work requires a different kind of emotional availability, being open to your own feelings, exploring difficult topics, allowing vulnerability on to the page.

This doesn't mean you become emotionally unavailable to others, but it does mean recognising that you have emotional needs too, and that creative expression is one way of meeting them.

Setting Boundaries Around Your Writing Time

Boundaries are not walls—they're gates with you as the gatekeeper. Setting boundaries around your writing time means being clear about when you're available for writing and when you're available for other demands. It means treating your creative time with the same respect you'd give any other important commitment.

The biggest boundary challenge for women transitioning from caretaker to creator is internal. We've been conditioned to believe that taking time for ourselves is selfish, especially when others need us. This conditioning runs so deep that even when we create writing time, we often sabotage it by feeling guilty or by allowing interruptions we wouldn't tolerate for other commitments.

If setting aside large blocks of time feels impossible, start with boundaries around micro-moments.

- For the next 20 minutes, I'm not available for non-emergency questions.

- During my morning coffee, I'm reading/writing, not discussing schedules.

- When my notebook is open, please don't interrupt unless someone is bleeding.

Keep in mind that the people in your life aren't mind readers. If you want to write every Saturday morning from eight to ten, tell them. If you need thirty minutes of quiet time when you get home from work, say so. Frame these boundaries positively: 'I'm excited about this new project I'm working on' rather than 'Leave me alone, I'm trying to write.'

When you start claiming time and space for yourself, the people around you may push back. This doesn't mean they don't love you or want you to be happy; it means they're used to having unlimited access to your attention and energy. Hold your boundaries kindly but firmly. Remember that you're modelling healthy self-care. Treat your writing appointments with yourself as seriously as you would a doctor's appointment or work meeting. Don't cancel on yourself unless there's a genuine emergency. Don't use your writing time to catch up on household tasks or return phone calls.

Finally, share your writing goals with someone who will support your boundaries rather than undermine them. This might be a writing friend, an online community, or a family member who understands the importance of your creative work.

Transforming Guilt Into Creative Fuel

Guilt is perhaps the biggest obstacle women face in transitioning from caretaker to creator. We feel guilty for taking time away from family, for pursuing something that doesn't directly benefit others, for investing in ourselves when there are always more pressing needs around us.

But what if guilt could become fuel rather than an obstacle? What if the very intensity of that emotion could power your creative work instead of stopping it?

Most creative guilt stems from the belief that your time and energy belong to others first, and to you only if there's anything left over. This belief is learned, not innate, and it can be unlearned. When you feel guilty about writing, ask yourself: 'Whose voice is this? What would I tell my daughter if she felt guilty about pursuing something important to her?'

Instead of seeing your writing time as something you're taking away from others, consider what you're giving. When you honour your creativity, you're modelling for other women (especially younger ones) that their creative expression matters too. You're showing your family that you're a complete person with interests and passions beyond caregiving. You're contributing your unique perspective to the world.

The most powerful writing comes from exploring the emotions that try to silence us. Write about the guilt. Examine it on the page. Where did it come from? What stories is it telling you? What would life look like if you didn't carry it? Guilt often contains information about our values and fears—mine it for creative material.

Let guilt motivate you to write more consistently, not less. If you feel guilty about the time you're taking, honour that time by using it well. Don't waste your precious writing minutes scrolling social media or organising your desk. Write. The guilt will feel more justified if your creative time is productive.

You can feel guilty about taking time for yourself AND joyful about your creative work. These emotions can coexist. Don't wait for the guilt to disappear before you start writing because it might never fully go away, and that's OK. Learn to write while carrying it, to create despite it, to let joy and guilt occupy the same space.

You don't have unlimited time to express what's inside you. The stories you're not telling, the insights you're not sharing, the creative work you're not doing will all die with you if you don't claim them. Is making everyone else comfortable worth that loss?

Writing Exercise

This exercise will help you assess your current caretaking load, identify opportunities for creative space, and develop a realistic plan for honouring both your responsibilities and your creative needs.

1: Caretaking Audit

List all the ways you currently provide care: emotional, physical and logistical. Include family members, friends, colleagues, community organisations, pets, and so on. Be specific:

- Daily caregiving tasks (meals, transportation, emotional support)
- Weekly responsibilities (cleaning, shopping, scheduling)
- Seasonal or occasional care (holidays, special events, crisis support)
- Mental/emotional labour (remembering birthdays, managing family dynamics, worrying about others).

Now, next to each item, write:

- E (Essential): this absolutely cannot be delegated or eliminated
- D (Delegatable): someone else could do this, possibly with training
- R (Reducible): this could be done less frequently or less intensively
- E (Eliminable): this isn't actually necessary; I do it from habit/guilt.

2: Time Treasure Hunt

For one week, keep a log of how you spend your time in thirty-minute blocks. At the end of the week, identify:

- Pockets of time that could be repurposed for writing
- Activities that don't align with your priorities
- Moments when you're waiting that could be used for creative thinking
- Time spent on activities others could do for themselves.

Look particularly for:

- The first or last 30 minutes of your day
- Time spent scrolling social media or watching TV you don't enjoy

- Commute time or waiting time
- Household tasks that could be streamlined or shared.

3: Boundary Blueprint

Design your ideal creative boundaries:

Daily boundaries: *Each day, I will protect _____ minutes for writing by _____.*

Weekly boundaries: *Each week, I will have _____ hours of uninterrupted creative time during _____.*

Communication boundaries: *I will let my family know about my writing time by saying: _____.*

Emergency boundaries: *The only reasons I will interrupt my writing time are: _____.*

4: Guilt Investigation

Write about your guilt around taking time for creative work:

- Complete this sentence 10 times: *I feel guilty about writing because …*
- Where did these beliefs come from? Whose voices do you hear?
- What would you tell your best friend if they expressed these same guilty thoughts?

- What would your life look like in 10 years if guilt continued to stop you from writing?
- What would your life look like if you wrote despite the guilt?

5: Integration Strategy

Create a specific plan for the next month:

Week 1: *I will write for _____ minutes every _____ (day/time) in _____ (location).*

Week 2: *I will add _____ to my writing practice.*

Week 3: *I will _____ (increase time, add a boundary, try a new location, etc.).*

Week 4: *I will evaluate what's working and adjust by _____.*

6: Support System

Identify who in your life:

- Will support your transition to making time for writing
- Might resist your new boundaries (plan how to handle this)

- Could help with some of your caretaking responsibilities
- Shares similar creative struggles (potential accountability partner).

Write one specific action you'll take this week to build support for your creative work.

7: Creative Manifesto

Write a letter to yourself explaining why your creative work matters, not just to you but to the world. Include:
- What unique perspective you bring to your writing
- How your caretaking experience informs your creativity
- What you want to model for other women
- What you might regret if you don't honour your creative calling.

Keep this manifesto somewhere you can read it when guilt or overwhelm threatens to derail your writing practice.

Remember: you're not choosing between being a caretaker and being a creator. You're expanding your identity to include both. This integration isn't selfish; it's necessary, not just for you, but for everyone who needs to see that women's creative work matters.

THE COMPARISON TRAP

> 'I spent an hour scrolling through Instagram, looking at writers half my age posting about their book deals and literary awards. I closed the app feeling like I'd missed some crucial deadline, like I was too late to the party that everyone else seemed to know about. Then I opened my manuscript and remembered: this isn't a race. It's my story, told in my time, in my voice.'
>
> – Rebecca

Social media has revolutionised how writers connect, promote their work, and build audiences. But for the midlife writer, these platforms can become a minefield of comparison and self-doubt. When your feed is filled with twenty-something debut novelists, writers celebrating their fifth published book, and endless posts about literary achievements, it's easy to feel like you're perpetually behind, perpetually too late, perpetually not enough.

The comparison trap is particularly cruel to women over fifty because it preys on our existing insecurities about age, relevance, and missed opportunities. But here's what social media doesn't show: the full story. Behind every celebration post are years of rejection, revision and doubt. Behind every 'overnight success' is often a decade of invisible work. And behind every young achiever is someone who hasn't yet lived enough life to write with the depth and wisdom that comes only with time.

Comparison has always been the thief of joy, but social media has made it systematic and unavoidable. Several factors make comparison especially damaging:

Publishing culture often celebrates young debuts as if youth itself were a literary achievement. While there's something inspiring about early success, the constant focus on '30 Under 30' lists and 'Young Writers to Watch' can make us feel invisible or irrelevant. This messaging ignores the fact that many of literature's greatest works were written by authors in their later years, when they had accumulated the wisdom and perspective that only comes with living.

Social media creates an illusion of constant productivity. Writers post about finishing drafts, landing agents, and publishing books with a frequency that can make your own progress feel glacial. The full timeline, the years of work that preceded the announcement, the projects that didn't work out, the long periods of apparent 'nothing' that are essential creative gestation.

People often share their successes, not their struggles. For every post about a book deal, there are dozens of unseen rejections. For every celebration of a positive review, there are silent disappointments. When you compare your internal experience (full of doubt and difficulty) to others' external presentations (curated success stories), you're comparing reality to illusion.

Social media can also make it feel like having a 'platform' is more important than having something to say. Writers worry about building followers before they've built their craft, about going viral before they've gone deep. This can be especially overwhelming for new writers who came of age in an era when good writing was enough—now it seems like good marketing is equally essential.

Online discussions about publishing can reinforce the false belief that there's limited space for new voices, that opportunities are scarce, that someone else's success diminishes your chances. In reality, readers are hungry for diverse perspectives, including those of women who've lived long enough to have something profound to say.

The antidote to comparison is creating your own definition of writing success, one that aligns with your values, circumstances and goals rather than with social media's narrow metrics of achievement. Traditional publishing metrics focus on external validation: book deals, bestseller lists, awards, reviews, follower counts. But these metrics may not reflect what matters to you as a writer. Before you can resist comparison, you need clarity about what success looks like for your unique situation and aspirations.

- Instead of focusing solely on outcomes (which are often beyond your control), consider celebrating process victories: completing a first draft, establishing a consistent writing routine, finishing a difficult chapter, or writing more honestly than you ever have before. These achievements are entirely within your control and build the foundation for whatever external success may follow.

- How has writing changed you? Are you more comfortable with vulnerability? More skilled at observation? Better at processing your experiences? These internal transformations are often more valuable than external recognition, but they're easy to overlook when you're focused on what others are achieving.

- Who has your writing touched? Maybe it's a single reader who told you your essay helped them feel less alone. Maybe it's your children or grandchildren who will someday treasure your stories. Maybe it's a writing group where your encouragement helped someone else find their voice. Impact doesn't require a large audience; it requires authentic connection.

- Are you becoming a better writer? Can you express complex emotions more clearly than you could last year? Do you trust your voice more? Are you taking creative risks that stretch your abilities? Craft development is a lifelong journey, and every writer has the advantage of life experience to draw from.

- Does writing bring you alive? Do you look forward to your writing time? Does the process of creation satisfy something essential in you, regardless of where the work goes afterwards? Joy is both an undervalued metric and perhaps the most important one; if your writing doesn't nourish you, external success will feel hollow.

- What are you leaving behind? This might be published work, but it might also be journals for your family, stories that preserve important memories, or simply the example of a woman who honoured her creative calling. Legacy success isn't about fame; it's about authenticity and completion.

The writing community you choose can either fuel comparison and insecurity or provide encouragement and perspective. Now you have the wisdom to be intentional about the creative community you cultivate.

Unfollow accounts that consistently make you feel inadequate. Seek out writers who share the messy realities of the creative process, who celebrate others generously, and who represent diverse paths to success. Look for accounts that focus on craft development, not just achievement announcements.

Instead of comparing yourself to writers decades younger, connect with others who share your stage of life. Join online groups for midlife writers, seek out local writing circles for women over fifty, or start your own group. There's something powerful about being around people who understand the unique challenges and advantages of writing later in life.

When you see another writer's success, practice responding with genuine celebration rather than comparison. This isn't about forcing fake positivity; it's about training yourself to see others' achievements as proof that good things are possible rather than evidence that opportunities are scarce. Picture yourself in their shoes; there they are putting themselves and their hard-earned work out into the ether hoping to catch someone's attention. A like, a smiley face, a simple comment can make someone's day and will connect you to other like-minded women.

If you use social media as a writer, consider sharing your process, not just your achievements. Talk about the difficult days, the revisions, the rejections alongside the celebrations. This honesty helps break the highlight reel illusion and gives others permission to be real about their own creative struggles.

Look for writers whose careers inspire you. Read their stories, learn from their paths. Simultaneously, be willing to encourage newer writers. Mentoring others reminds you of how far you've come and helps combat the scarcity mindset. Join communities that focus on craft development and creative growth rather than marketing and promotion.

Writing Exercise

This exercise will help you identify your personal definition of writing success and develop strategies for building a supportive creative community.

1: Success Archaeology

Think back to moments in your life when you felt truly successful—not necessarily in writing, but in any area. These might be small moments that no one else noticed or major achievements that were celebrated. For each memory, identify:

- What made this feel like success to you?
- Who (if anyone) witnessed or validated this success?
- How did this success align with your values?
- What internal qualities did this success reflect?

Now write about patterns you notice. What kinds of success have historically felt most meaningful to you? How might these patterns inform your definition of writing success?

2: Your Personal Success Manifesto

Create your own definition of writing success by completing these statements:

I will consider my writing successful when:

- I have _____ (process goal)
- I feel _____ (emotional goal)
- I have created _____ (craft goal)
- I have shared _____ (impact goal)
- I have honoured _____ (values goal).

Success does NOT require:

- (List external markers that you're releasing: publication, awards, income, followers, etc.)

I will celebrate:

- Small victories like _____
- Progress indicators like _____
- Personal growth like _____.

Write this manifesto as a letter to yourself, explaining why these metrics matter more than external validation.

3: Comparison Audit

For the next week, pay attention to when you feel comparison creeping in. Keep a simple log:

- What triggered the comparison?
- What story did you tell yourself in that moment?
- How did the comparison make you feel?
- What would you tell a friend experiencing the same comparison?

At the end of the week, look for patterns. Are there particular platforms, types of content, or times of day when comparison hits hardest?

4: Community Curation

Assess your current writing community:

Online community audit:

- Which social media accounts consistently inspire vs deflate you?
- Which writing-related content makes you excited to write vs makes you want to quit?
- What adjustments can you make to your feed to support your creative goals?

Offline community assessment:

- Who in your life supports your writing goals?
- Who understands the challenges of creative work at midlife?
- Where could you find more supportive creative community?

Community building plan:

- One account you'll unfollow this week
- One new positive influence you'll seek out
- One way you'll contribute to others' creative journeys
- One step towards finding more supportive offline community.

5: Celebration Practice

List ten writing-related things you've accomplished in the past year that deserve celebration, no matter how small:

- Pages written
- Writing sessions completed
- Creative risks taken
- Honest moments captured

- Skills developed
- Connections made
- Ideas explored
- Voice trusted
- Time claimed
- Joy experienced.

Choose one of these accomplishments and write yourself a proper congratulations note. Practice celebrating your own creative journey.

6: Response Strategy

Develop a toolkit for moments when comparison threatens to derail you:

When I see someone else's success and feel inadequate, I will:

1. Take 3 deep breaths and remind myself that _____
2. Look at my success manifesto and remember that _____
3. Do one small writing-related thing to reconnect with my own creative journey.
4. If needed, step away from social media and _____.

My mantras for comparison moments:

- There is room for all our stories.
- My timeline is not their timeline.
- I am writing my story, not competing in their race.
- (Add your own).

7: Community Contribution

Identify one specific way you'll contribute to a more supportive writing community this month:

- Celebrating someone else's achievement genuinely
- Sharing something honest about your own creative process
- Offering encouragement to another writer
- Starting a conversation about the realities of midlife creativity.

Remember: the goal isn't to never feel comparison—it's to recognise it quickly and have tools to return to your own creative path. Every moment you spend focused on someone else's journey is a moment you're not investing in your own story.

WORKING WITH MEMORY

> 'I sat down to write about my mother's death ten years ago, but what came out was the smell of her lavender soap and the way she hummed while folding laundry when I was seven. Memory doesn't follow chronology—it follows the heart. I'm learning to trust that and follow where it leads, even when it takes me somewhere I didn't plan to go.'
>
> – Catherine

Memory is the writer's most abundant resource and most complex challenge. By the time we reach our middle years, we carry decades of experiences, relationships, losses and insights, a vast archive of material that younger writers simply haven't had time to accumulate. But memory isn't a filing cabinet where experiences are stored in neat chronological order. It's more like an ocean where events float at different depths, surfacing unexpectedly, shifting with the tides of emotion and association, sometimes crystal clear and sometimes frustratingly murky.

What neuroscience now reveals is that your ageing brain isn't just storing more memories; it's developing sophisticated systems for accessing and connecting them in ways that serve creative work. The bilateral processing that increases with age allows you to engage both analytical and intuitive thinking simultaneously when exploring memories. Your crystallised intelligence, and the accumulated knowledge and patterns stored over decades, now create rich networks of association that younger writers haven't yet developed.

Learning to work with memory as a creative tool means understanding both its gifts and its limitations. It means developing techniques for diving deep into the past while writing from the perspective of who you are now. It means accepting that memory is subjective, selective, and sometimes unreliable and discovering that these very qualities can enhance rather than diminish your creative work.

The Neuroscience of Memory and Age

Recent research reveals that the mature brain processes memories differently than younger brains, in ways that enhance creative potential. As we age, our brains develop stronger connections between hemispheres, allowing for more integrated access to stored experiences. This bilateral processing means you can simultaneously access the emotional resonance of a memory (typically right-brain processing) while organising it into a coherent narrative (typically left-brain processing) (Perera, 2024).

Your crystallised intelligence represents decades of

Working with Memory

accumulated knowledge, patterns, and connections stored in your neural networks. Unlike fluid intelligence, which peaks in youth, crystallised intelligence continues to grow throughout life. This means your ability to see patterns, make connections between seemingly unrelated experiences, and understand the deeper significance of events improves with age.

When you write from memory now, you're drawing from this vast network of crystallised intelligence. A single sensory detail such as the smell of your grandmother's kitchen can activate multiple memory networks simultaneously: emotional memories of feeling loved and safe, cultural memories of family traditions, historical memories of how daily life was different then, and philosophical insights about the passage of time. This rich associative capacity allows for layered, complex writing that captures both specific details and universal themes.

The mature brain's enhanced bilateral processing also means you can maintain what we might call 'emotional distance with intimate access'. You can revisit difficult memories while simultaneously processing them with the wisdom and perspective you've gained since they occurred. This dual capacity allows for writing that is both emotionally honest and psychologically sophisticated.

Our brains are remarkable archival systems, but accessing long-term memories for creative work often requires more than simply thinking, 'What happened that day?' Memories are stored through multiple pathways: sensory, emotional, narrative and associative. The key to rich recall is engaging as many of these pathways as possible. Your crystallised intelligence has organised decades of experiences into interconnected networks. When you activate one memory pathway, it naturally connects to related memories, creating the kind of rich, layered recall that produces compelling writing. This is why a single sensory trigger can unlock entire landscapes of memory that seemed forgotten.

Sensory Pathways to Memory

Our senses often hold the keys to the deepest memories, and your mature brain has developed sophisticated networks connecting sensory experiences across decades. The smell of certain flowers might instantly transport you to your grandmother's garden, but now your bilateral processing allows you to simultaneously access the emotional comfort of that memory, analyse what made that relationship special, and understand how it shaped your values about family and home.

When you want to access memories from a particular period, try focusing on:

- **Smells:** what did your childhood home smell like? Your first apartment? The hospital when your children were born. Your crystallised intelligence has stored thousands of scent associations that can unlock detailed memory networks.

- **Sounds:** what music was playing during important periods of your life? What voices, machines, natural sounds formed the soundtrack of different eras? Your mature brain can now recognise how these auditory memories connect to broader cultural and personal themes.

- **Textures:** the fabric of a favourite dress, the smoothness of a banister you slid down as a child, the roughness of your father's hands. Physical memories often carry the strongest emotional associations because they're processed through multiple brain regions simultaneously.

- **Tastes:** holiday foods, the cafeteria lunch that made you homesick, the cake at your wedding. Taste memories often unlock entire social and cultural contexts that your accumulated knowledge can now interpret with sophistication.

Start with one sensory detail and let your brain's associative networks take over. Don't force a narrative, just follow the sensory thread and trust your crystallised intelligence to reveal the connections and patterns that make memories meaningful.

One of the greatest advantages you have now as a writer is the ability to write about experiences with the understanding that comes only from time and perspective. This isn't just about having more experiences to draw from; it's about having the emotional and intellectual tools to make sense of those experiences in ways that weren't possible when they first occurred.

Your bilateral processing allows you to maintain what we might call 'double vision'—that is seeing events both as you experienced them then and as you understand them now. This layered perspective creates rich, complex narratives that honour both the innocence or confusion of your younger self and the wisdom of your current understanding. Your crystallised intelligence now recognises patterns that were invisible when you were living through events. You can see the thread of resilience that runs through seemingly separate experiences, understand family dynamics that puzzled you as a child, or recognise how seemingly random events were part of larger themes in your life. This pattern recognition, enhanced by decades of accumulated knowledge, allows you to write with a narrative sophistication that comes only from the long view.

Memory is not a video recording; it's a creative act that happens each time we remember. Every time we access a memory, we subtly reshape it, influenced by our current emotions, knowledge and needs. Your mature brain's enhanced processing helps you work more effectively with imperfect memories. Bilateral processing allows you to simultaneously acknowledge uncertainty while exploring emotional truth. Your crystallised intelligence helps you fill in gaps not with random invention but with informed understanding of how people behave, how relationships really work, and what the social context of past eras was like.

When writing from memory, distinguish between different types of truth:

- Factual truth: what actually happened, as it could be verified by external evidence
- Emotional truth: how events felt to you, then and now
- Narrative truth: how events fit into the larger story of your life and meaning-making
- Thematic truth: what events reveal about universal human experiences.

Creative writing often prioritises emotional, narrative and thematic truth over strict factual accuracy. Your accumulated wisdom helps you recognise which details matter for the story you're telling, and which can be gracefully approximated or imaginatively reconstructed.

Instead of seeing memory gaps as problems to solve, consider them as creative opportunities. When you can't remember exactly what someone said, you can focus on the emotional impact of their words. When you can't recall precise details, you can emphasise the sensory impressions and emotional truths that remain.

Your crystallised intelligence provides a rich context for creative reconstruction. You understand how people spoke in different eras, what daily life was like, and how historical events affected ordinary families. This accumulated knowledge allows you to fill memory gaps with informed imagination rather than random invention. Sometimes what you don't remember is as significant as what you do. The fact that certain details have faded while others remain vivid tells its own story about what mattered most, what had a lasting impact, and what your psyche needed to preserve or release.

Memory as Raw Material for Fiction

While memoir draws directly from your lived experiences, fiction allows you to transform your memories into new forms that can explore different possibilities and reach different audiences. Your crystallised intelligence and bilateral processing provide tremendous advantages for this transformation.

Your years of observing human behaviour have created vast networks of understanding about how people think, feel and react under different circumstances. When you write fiction, you're not inventing personalities from scratch; you're drawing from this rich database of observed patterns. The way your mother deflected difficult conversations, your colleague's habit of taking credit for others' work, your neighbour's unexpected generosity during crises, these behavioural observations can become authentic character traits for fictional people in completely different circumstances.

The key to using memory for fiction is emotional transformation rather than factual transcription. Take the emotional core of an experience but change the external circumstances. For instance, the grief you felt when your marriage ended contains universal truths about loss, identity shift, and rebuilding that could inform a fictional character's response to job loss, friendship betrayal, or any other significant ending. Your bilateral processing allows you to access the authentic emotional landscape while your crystallised intelligence helps you imagine how that same emotional truth might manifest in different circumstances.

Your family of origin provided you with a master class in human psychology and relationship dynamics. Even if you don't want to write directly about your family, you can use what you learned about how people function in intimate relationships to create believable fictional families. Your accumulated understanding of how birth order affects personality, how family secrets shape behaviour, how people repeat or rebel against generational patterns, and how love can coexist with frustration is all there to help you create authentic fictional relationships.

The beauty of fiction is that you can explore 'what-if' scenarios safely. What if that difficult parent had been a boss instead of a family member? What if that family crisis had happened to strangers in a different culture? What if that moment of personal growth had occurred under completely different circumstances? Your memory provides the emotional authenticity while imagination provides the creative freedom.

Writing Exercise

This exercise will help you develop techniques for accessing deep memories and transforming them into compelling creative material while navigating the complexities of unreliable recall.

1: Sensory Memory Mapping

Choose a significant period from your past (a particular year, a season, a living situation). Create a sensory map by writing down:

- Smells: 5 to 10 scents from this period
- Sounds: background noises, voices, music, mechanical sounds
- Textures: fabrics, surfaces, objects you touched regularly
- Tastes: regular foods, special occasion foods, medicine, treats
- Visual details: colours, light quality, recurring images.

Now choose the sensory detail that feels most emotionally charged. Write for ten minutes, starting with that detail and following wherever it leads. Don't worry about chronology or narrative structure—just follow the sensory thread.

2: Photograph Deep Dive

Find a photograph from at least twenty years ago that includes people important to you. Study it for two to three minutes without writing, noticing everything you can.

Now write about this photograph using the 'double vision' approach:

- First 10 minutes: write about what you see in the photo from the perspective of who you were then. What were you thinking and feeling in that moment? What was important to you? What were you unaware of?
- Next 10 minutes: write about the same photograph from your current perspective. What do you see now that you didn't see then? What has changed? What patterns do you recognise?
- Final 5 minutes: write about what the photograph represents in the larger story of your life.

3: Dialogue Across Time

Choose a difficult or confusing period from your past. Write a conversation between your current self and your past self during that time. Let your current self offer perspective, comfort, or wisdom to your younger self. Let your younger self ask questions or express frustrations. Notice what each version of yourself understands that the other doesn't.

4: Memory Reconstruction Exercise

Think of an important conversation from your past—one that affected you deeply but whose exact words you can't remember. This might be:

- A difficult conversation with a parent
- An important talk with a mentor
- A breakup or reconciliation
- A moment of receiving significant news.

Write this conversation as a scene, acknowledging that you're reconstructing rather than transcribing. Focus on:

- The emotional temperature of the conversation
- The physical setting and your bodily sensations
- The essence of what was communicated, even if not the exact words
- How the conversation felt to you both during and after.

At the beginning of your scene, write a brief note acknowledging the creative reconstruction: 'I can't remember exactly what she said, but the conversation went something like this …' or 'The words aren't precise, but the feeling was …'

5: Collaborative Memory Investigation

Identify someone who shared significant experiences with you during a period you're interested in writing about. This could be a sibling, childhood friend, former colleague, or long-term partner.

Write out:

- Three specific questions you'd like to ask them about shared memories
- What you hope to discover or confirm
- How you might handle differences in your recollections
- Whether you want to interview them for creative material or just for personal understanding.

If appropriate, reach out and have this conversation. If that's not possible, write what you imagine their responses might be and how those imagined responses compare to your own memories.

6: Truth Inventory

Choose a memory you've been wanting to write about. Analyse it through different lenses:

Factual truth: What facts can you verify? What details are you uncertain about?

Emotional truth: How did this experience feel? How does it feel now when you remember it?

Narrative truth: How does this experience fit into the larger story of your life? What does it reveal about your character, growth or patterns?

Thematic truth: What universal human experiences does this memory illustrate? How might it resonate with others?

Write a paragraph about this memory emphasising each type of truth. Notice how different emphases create different versions of the same experience.

7: Memory Manifesto

Write yourself a permission slip for working with imperfect memories:

- I give myself permission to write from memory even when I can't remember everything perfectly because …

- I understand that my memories are shaped by my perspective, and that makes them …
- When I can't recall exact details, I will …
- I trust my emotional memory because …
- The story I tell about my past serves the purpose of …

Remember: your memories aren't historical documents—they're creative material. They've been shaped by time, emotion and perspective into something uniquely yours. Trust the story your memory wants to tell, even when—especially when—it's imperfect.

HONOURING YOUR BODY'S WISDOM

'I used to think I could write anywhere, anytime—pulling all-nighters, hunched over my laptop for hours, fuelled by coffee and determination. Now my body has different requirements. My back demands a proper chair, my eyes need better light, my brain functions best in the morning when my hormones aren't wreaking havoc. At first, I resented these limitations. Then I realised they weren't limitations—they were invitations to write more mindfully, more sustainably, and ultimately more successfully.'

– Maria

The relationship between body and creativity shifts significantly over time, and these changes require both acceptance and adaptation. Your body may not have the same stamina it once did, but it offers compensations: deeper sensory awareness, a richer understanding of physical experience, and the wisdom that comes from inhabiting a body that has lived, loved, laboured and endured.

Too often, we approach the physical changes of life as deficits to overcome rather than information to incorporate. But your changing body isn't betraying your creative work; it is teaching you new ways to approach it. Learning to write in partnership with your physical self, rather than in spite of it, can enhance both your creative process and your written work.

One of the most noticeable changes many women experience is a shift in energy patterns. The ability to power through fatigue, to work at any hour, to sustain focus regardless of physical comfort diminishes. Initially, this can feel like a creative failure, but let's view it as an invitation to work more strategically and sustainably.

Your body has its own circadian rhythms, and these may become more pronounced with age. Some women discover they're naturally most creative in the early morning, when cortisol levels are high and the world is quiet. Others find their peak creative hours in the afternoon or evening. Pay attention to when your mind feels sharpest, when ideas flow most easily, when concentration comes naturally.

This isn't about forcing yourself into a predetermined schedule; it's about discovering your body's preferences and designing your writing practice around them. If you're a natural early bird, protect your morning hours for writing, even if it means saying no to early meetings or social commitments. If you're more creative in the evening, don't feel guilty about not being a morning writer.

Traditional productivity advice focuses on time

Honouring Your Body's Wisdom

management, but some writers often benefit more from energy management. You might have three hours available for writing, but only ninety minutes of high-quality mental energy. Learning to recognise and honour these energy cycles allows you to use your peak moments for the most demanding creative work.

Consider keeping an energy log for a week, noting not just when you feel tired or alert, but when you feel creatively energised, emotionally available, and mentally sharp. Look for patterns related to sleep, meals, exercise, stress levels, and hormonal cycles. Use this information to schedule your most important writing during your personal peak hours.

Physical changes might mean you can't write for six hours straight anymore, but this isn't necessarily a loss. Shorter, more focused writing sessions can be more productive than lengthy periods of diminishing returns. The pressure to finish this chapter today can give way to a more sustainable approach that honours both your creative process and your physical needs.

Many successful authors discover that limitations breed creativity. When you only have an hour to write, you waste less time on social media. When your back hurts after sitting too long, you learn to think while walking. When your eyes tire from screens, you might rediscover the pleasure of writing by hand.

Some writers find they're better at generating new material during high-energy phases and editing during lower-energy periods. Others discover that emotional vulnerability during certain times leads to more honest, powerful writing. Track your patterns and experiment with matching different types of creative work to different energy states.

Creating a sustainable writing practice may require practical adaptations. Don't view these adaptations as concessions to ageing; see them as optimisations to improve both your comfort and your creativity.

- **Ergonomic considerations:** physical discomfort is creativity's enemy. If your neck hurts, your back aches, or your wrists are strained, part of your mental energy goes to managing pain instead of generating ideas. Investing in your physical comfort is investing in your creative output. Consider your writing setup: is your screen at eye level to prevent neck strain? Does your chair support your lower back? Are your feet flat on the floor? Do you have adequate lighting that doesn't strain your eyes? These might seem like minor details, but they can significantly impact your ability to sustain focus and enjoy the writing process.

- **Movement:** sitting for long periods becomes increasingly uncomfortable with age, but this doesn't mean you have to abandon extended writing sessions. Instead, build movement into your creative process. Some writers set timers to remind themselves to stand and stretch every 30 minutes. Others discover that walking stimulates creative thinking and carry notebooks or voice recorders for capturing ideas on the move. Consider experimenting with different writing positions: standing desks, balance balls, comfortable chairs with ottomans, or even writing in bed with proper support. The goal is to find positions that allow you to think clearly without physical distraction.

- **Vision and lighting:** poor lighting can cause eye strain, headaches and fatigue. Ensure your writing space has adequate lighting, preferably natural light during the day and warm, sufficient artificial light in the evening. Consider adjusting font sizes on your computer to reduce eye strain, and don't hesitate to use reading glasses if they help. Some writers discover that certain times of day are better for screen work while others are better for handwritten work.

- **Technology adaptations:** if typing becomes uncomfortable, explore voice-to-text software, ergonomic keyboards, or dictation tools. These tools can liberate your creativity by removing physical barriers to expression. Some writers find that alternating between handwriting and typing reduces strain while also engaging different parts of their creative process. Handwriting often feels more intimate and can access different types of thinking than typing.

Using Sensory Awareness

Your body has accumulated decades of sensory experience. You know how different fabrics feel against the skin, how various climates affect mood and energy, how the light changes throughout seasons and years. This embodied knowledge becomes a rich resource for creating authentic, detailed writing. Draw on your body's memory bank: How does anxiety feel different from excitement in your chest? What does grief do to your posture? How does joy change your breathing? This somatic awareness can add layers of authenticity to both fiction and nonfiction writing.

Mindfulness practices can enhance both your physical comfort and your sensory awareness while writing. Before beginning a writing session, spend a few minutes noticing your body: How are you sitting? What do you smell, hear, feel? What's the temperature, the light quality, the energy in the room? This practice serves multiple purposes: it grounds you in the present moment, helps you notice and address physical discomfort before it becomes distracting, and attunes you to sensory details you might incorporate into your writing.

Are you sensitive to your physical environment? To noise, lighting, temperature and clutter. If you've become more sensitive to noise, invest in noise-cancelling headphones or seek quieter writing spaces. If clutter distracts you more than it used to, create a cleaner, more organised writing environment. If certain scents or lighting conditions enhance your mood and creativity, incorporate them into your writing ritual.

Your body's response to seasons and weather patterns may have become more pronounced with age. Use this awareness to inform your writing practice and subject matter. Write about storms while listening to rain, explore themes of renewal during spring, or examine loss and letting go during autumn. Some writers discover they're more introspective during certain seasons, more energetic during others, or more emotionally available during specific weather patterns. Track these connections and use them strategically in your creative work.

Let your body's responses guide your writing topics and approaches. If you notice tension in your shoulders, explore what you might be carrying metaphysically. If you feel expansiveness in your chest, investigate what's creating that openness. Physical sensations can be doorways into emotional and psychological material. This practice can be particularly powerful when writing about characters' internal experiences or for exploring your own emotional landscape in memoir or personal essay work.

Writing Exercise

This exercise will help you assess your current physical relationship with writing and develop strategies for creating a more sustainable, comfortable, and sensory-rich writing practice.

1: Body Awareness Inventory

Spend a week tracking your physical experience while writing. Each day, note:

Energy patterns:

- What time did you feel most mentally alert?
- When did creative ideas flow most easily?
- What time of day felt most challenging for focus?
- How did your energy change throughout your writing session?

Physical comfort:

- What parts of your body felt uncomfortable while writing?

- How long could you maintain focus before physical discomfort became distracting?
- What environmental factors (light, temperature, noise) affected your comfort?
- Did certain positions or setups work better than others?

Sensory environment:

- What did you notice about sounds, smells, textures, lighting?
- Which sensory elements enhanced your creativity vs distracted from it?
- How did your sensory awareness change during different types of writing tasks?

At the end of the week, identify patterns and areas for improvement.

2: Energy Optimisation Plan

Based on your tracking, create a personalised energy management strategy:

- My peak creative hours are: _____
- During these hours, I will protect time for: (new writing, complex editing, difficult scenes, etc.)

- My moderate energy hours are: _____
- During these hours, I can do: (routine editing, research, correspondence, etc.)
- My low energy hours are: _____
- During these hours, I might: (read for inspiration, organise files, plan future projects, rest)
- To honour my energy patterns, I will:
    o Schedule my most important writing during _____

    o Say no to _____ during my peak hours

    o Prepare for writing sessions by _____

    o Recognise when I need breaks by noticing _____.

3: Physical Comfort Assessment

Evaluate and improve your writing environment:

Current setup evaluation:

- Rate your current chair, desk height, lighting, and screen position (1–10)
- Identify the biggest physical discomfort you experience while writing.
- Note how long you can comfortably write before needing to move.

Immediate improvements I can make:

- Lighting adjustments
- Seating modifications
- Screen positioning
- Addition of cushions, footrests, or other supports.

Movement integration plan:

- Set a timer to remind myself to move every _____ minutes.
- During breaks, I will _____ (stretch, walk, do specific movements)
- I will experiment with writing while _____ (standing, walking, in different locations).

Investment priorities:

- If I could improve one thing about my physical writing setup, it would be _____.
- The next purchase I'll make to support my writing comfort is _____.

4: Sensory Writing Enhancement

Sensory environment design: create an ideal sensory environment for writing:

- What scents enhance your creativity or calm your nervous system?
- What sounds or silence work best for different types of writing?
- What lighting conditions make you feel most alert and comfortable?
- What textures or objects comfort you or inspire creativity?

Design a ritual for preparing your sensory environment before writing.

Somatic awareness practice: before your next writing session, spend five minutes doing a body scan:

- Notice tension, comfort, energy, temperature.
- Observe your breathing, posture, facial expression.
- Identify any emotions held in your body.

Then write for ten minutes about whatever your body scan revealed.

5: Seasonal and Cyclical Planning

Personal rhythm recognition:

- Do you notice energy or mood changes related to seasons, weather, or (if applicable) menstrual cycles?
- Are there times of year when you feel more creative, introspective or energetic?
- How do major weather events (storms, temperature changes, light changes) affect your creativity?

Cyclical writing strategy:

- Plan different types of writing projects for different seasons or energy cycles.
- Identify which creative tasks work best during various physical/emotional states.
- Create a flexible yearly writing plan that honours your natural rhythms.

6: Adaptive Technology and Tools

Consider tools that might support your physical writing practice:

- Voice-to-text software for when typing is uncomfortable

- Ergonomic keyboards or writing tools
- Apps that remind you to take breaks or do eye exercises
- Standing desk converters or writing surfaces
- Blue light filters or computer glasses.

Choose one new tool or adaptation to try this month.

7: Physical Self-Care Integration

Develop a holistic approach to supporting your writing through physical care:

Before writing:

- How will you prepare your body for creative work? (stretching, breathing, movement)

During writing:

- What signals will tell you when you need a break?
- How will you maintain physical comfort during longer sessions?

After writing:

- How will you care for your body after intense creative work?

- What practices help you transition out of writing mode?

Daily/weekly support:

- What physical practices support your overall creative energy? (exercise, sleep, nutrition, stress management)

8: Embodied Writing Practice

Try writing a piece that directly incorporates your physical experience:

Choose one of these approaches:

- Write about a memory using primarily sensory details from your body's perspective.
- Describe a current emotion by focusing on how it feels in your body.
- Create a character's experience by writing from their physical sensations.
- Explore a place by describing how your body responded to being there.

Focus on specificity: not just 'I felt sad' but 'My chest felt hollow, my shoulders curved inwards, my breathing became shallow.'

Remember: your body's challenges are not an obstacle to overcome; it's a partner in your creative process. Learning to work with your physical self rather than against it can lead to a more sustainable, enjoyable, and ultimately more successful writing practice. Your embodied experience is also a rich source of authentic detail that can make your writing more vivid and relatable.

ALCHEMISING LOSS AND GRIEF

'After my husband died, I couldn't write for months. Words felt too small, too inadequate for the vastness of what I was feeling. When I finally put pen to paper again, what came out wasn't pretty or polished—it was raw and real and necessary.'

– Susan

In our lives we will all become intimate with loss. We may have buried parents, ended marriages, watched children leave home, lost jobs that we felt defined us, said goodbye to dreams that didn't materialise, and felt our own bodies change in ways that remind us of our mortality. We've experienced the grief of watching friends struggle with illness, of losing mentors who shaped us, of witnessing a world that seems increasingly fragile and uncertain.

These losses can feel like endings: of relationships, chapters, possibilities. But as a writer, loss can also be a beginning: the beginning of deeper wisdom, more authentic expression, and writing that speaks to the universal human experience of impermanence and resilience. Learning to transform grief into art isn't about prettifying pain or finding silver linings where none exist. It's about discovering that our most difficult experiences can become our most powerful teachers and our most important stories.

Major losses will often coincide with significant life transitions: retirement, empty nest, divorce, death of parents, health crises. These transitions can feel like identity earthquakes, shaking the foundations of who we thought we were and forcing us to reconstruct our sense of self.

Anthropologists refer to the space between identities as 'liminal'. The threshold space where we're no longer who we were but haven't yet become who we're going to be. This can be terrifying, but it's also where transformation happens. Liminal spaces are incredibly fertile for writing because they strip away familiar roles and defences, revealing essential truths about who we are beneath our social identities. When you're amid major transition, resist the urge to rush towards a new identity or to cling to an old one. Instead, lean into the uncertainty. Write from the place of not knowing. Some of the most powerful writing emerges from the honest exploration of confusion, fear and possibility that characterises transitional periods.

Major losses often require us to excavate our identities, separating what was truly ours from what belonged to roles we played or relationships we inhabited. When you lose a marriage, you might discover parts of yourself that were suppressed during the relationship. When children leave home, you might rediscover interests and passions that were set aside during intensive parenting years. When you retire, you might question who you are beyond your professional identity. This identity archaeology is rich material for writing. Document the process of rediscovering yourself. Write about the person you were before you became wife, mother, caregiver, professional. Write about the dreams you deferred and whether they still call to you. Write about the surprising things you're learning about yourself in the absence of familiar structures.

Loss often involves the shattering of illusions about relationships, about fairness, about control, about permanence. While disillusionment is painful, it's also liberating. When illusions fall away, we see more clearly. We become less naive and more wise, less idealistic and more realistic, less protected and more authentic.

Write about your disillusionments not as failures but as education. What did you believe about love, life, family, work, ageing that you now know to be incomplete or untrue? How has the loss of these illusions changed your perspective? What wisdom have you gained that you wish you could share with your younger self or with others facing similar disillusionments? One of the most profound ways humans cope with loss is through meaning-making, which is the process of creating narrative coherence from experiences that initially feel senseless or overwhelming. Writing is one of the most powerful tools for this kind of meaning-making because it allows us to experiment with different ways of understanding our experiences.

Every loss involves multiple possible narratives. The death

of a parent might be a story about medical failure, family dysfunction, the unfairness of life, the circle of generations, the power of love, or the importance of forgiveness. The end of a marriage might be a story about personal failure, incompatibility, growth in different directions, or liberation from an unhealthy dynamic. The story you choose to tell yourself and others, shapes how you experience the loss. This doesn't mean choosing false optimism or denying pain. It means recognising that you have some agency in how you frame your experiences, and that different framings can lead to different emotional and psychological outcomes.

Many loss narratives move through predictable stages. Initially, we may see ourselves as victims of circumstances beyond our control. With time and processing, we might shift to seeing ourselves as survivors who endured difficult experiences. Eventually, we may recognise ourselves as thrivers who not only survived but were somehow enhanced by working through loss. Writing can help facilitate this progression by allowing you to explore different narrative perspectives. Write your loss story from the victim perspective where you are honestly acknowledging the unfairness, the pain, the things that were beyond your control. Then try writing it from the survivor perspective where you are focusing on your resilience, the help you received, the ways you coped. Finally, attempt the thriver perspective where you are exploring what you learned, how you grew, what became possible because of what you endured.

One of the most powerful aspects of writing about loss is discovering how your specific experiences connect to

Alchemising Loss and Grief

universal human themes. Your grief becomes a window into the shared human experience of impermanence, love, resilience and mortality. This connection between the personal and the universal allows readers to find their own experiences reflected in your stories. When writing about loss, look for the universal themes embedded in your specific experience. A story about losing a parent might explore themes of generational love, the cycle of life and death, or the complex mixture of grief and relief that can accompany the end of suffering. A story about divorce might examine themes of forgiveness, the evolution of love, or the courage required to start over.

Writing about loss and grief requires particular skills because difficult emotions can overwhelm narrative structure, leaving us with pages of raw feeling but little shape or meaning. Learning to channel intense emotions into effective writing is both an artistic and a healing practice:

- When emotions feel too large or chaotic to write about directly, create a container for them. A metaphor, image or structure that can hold the intensity while giving it shape. You might imagine your grief as an ocean, your anger as a fire, your confusion as a fog. Once you have a controlling image, you can explore its qualities, its changes over time, its effects on the landscape around it.

- Instead of trying to capture the full intensity of difficult emotions, try examining them like archaeologists study artefacts. What does your anger look like? What colour is it? Does it have texture, temperature, weight? What triggers it? How does it move through your body? This kind of detailed observation can transform overwhelming emotion into manageable material.

- Sometimes writing about loss in the third person ('She felt …') creates enough distance to explore painful experiences without being overwhelmed by them. This technique allows you to access empathy for yourself as a character while maintaining enough emotional safety to continue writing.

- Try writing conversations between yourself and your emotions. Let grief speak in its own voice. What does it want you to know? What is it protecting you from? What does it need from you? This technique can reveal the wisdom hidden within difficult emotions and help you develop a more collaborative relationship with them.

- Develop a part of yourself that can observe and describe your emotional experience without being consumed by it. This witness voice is compassionate but not dramatic, honest but not self-pitying. It can say, 'Today the sadness felt like lead in my chest' without needing to elaborate on how unfair that is or how much it hurts.

- Difficult emotions often need to be approached in small doses. Instead of trying to write the whole story of a major loss in one sitting, commit to writing about it for just 10 to 15 minutes at a time. This prevents emotional overwhelm while still allowing you to make progress on processing and articulating your experience.

Before and after writing about difficult topics, use physical practices to ground yourself in the present moment. This might be deep breathing, gentle movement, holding a comforting object, or stepping outside. Remember you are a whole person who needs care during difficult emotional work.

Writing Exercise

This exercise will guide you through the process of exploring a significant loss and transforming it into meaningful creative work while caring for your emotional well-being throughout the process.

1: Loss Inventory

Create a gentle inventory of significant losses in your life. These might include:

- Deaths of people important to you
- Divorces or relationship endings
- Job losses or career changes
- Health changes or diagnoses
- Dreams that didn't materialise
- Homes or places that were important to you
- Changes in family dynamics
- Loss of roles or identities.

For each loss, note:

- Approximately when it occurred
- Whether you've processed it primarily alone or with support
- How much you've written or talked about it
- Your current relationship to this loss (raw, healing, integrated, avoidant).

Choose one loss that feels ready for creative exploration and is significant enough to matter but not so raw that writing about it feels unsafe.

2: Narrative Perspective Exploration

Write about your chosen loss from three different narrative perspectives:

- The victim story: write about this loss focusing on its unfairness, the pain it caused, what was taken from you, how powerless you felt. Be honest about the genuine damage and difficulty. This isn't self-pity; it's acknowledgement of real harm.
- The survivor story: write about the same loss focusing on how you coped, what helped you through it, evidence of your resilience, support you received, ways you protected yourself or others during the difficult time.

- The wisdom story: write about what this loss taught you, how it changed your perspective, unexpected gifts that emerged from it, ways it connected you to others or to deeper truths about life. This doesn't minimise the pain but explores what grew from it.

Notice which perspective feels most natural to you and which feels most challenging.

3: Emotional Archaeology

Choose the most complex emotion connected to your loss (grief, anger, relief, guilt, fear, etc.). Spend fifteen minutes examining this emotion as if you were a scientist studying an interesting specimen:

- What does this emotion look like, feel like, sound like?
- Where do you feel it in your body?
- How has it changed over time?
- What triggers it now?
- What makes it soften or intensify?
- If this emotion could speak, what would it say?
- What does this emotion want you to understand?

Then spend five minutes writing a brief dialogue between yourself and this emotion.

4: Universal Connection

Identify the universal human themes embedded in your personal loss:

- What does your experience reveal about love, mortality, resilience, change?
- How might someone with a completely different loss still relate to your experience?
- What would you want others facing similar losses to know?
- What aspects of your experience feel uniquely yours vs broadly human?

Write a paragraph addressing someone else who might be facing a similar loss, sharing the wisdom you've gained without minimising their pain.

5: Container Creation

Create an extended metaphor or controlling image for your loss experience.

This might be:

- A natural phenomenon (storm, earthquake, drought, flood)

- A journey (through wilderness, foreign country, maze)
- A physical structure (bridge, house, wall, garden)
- A body of water (ocean, river, pond, waterfall).

Develop this metaphor in detail. How does your loss resemble this image? How has the 'landscape' changed over time? What does the metaphor reveal about your experience that direct description might miss?

Write now about where you are now in this metaphorical landscape.

6: Meaning-Making Draft

Using insights from the previous exercises, write a complete piece about your loss that includes:

- Honest acknowledgement of the pain and difficulty
- Recognition of your resilience and coping
- Connection to universal human experiences
- Some sense of meaning or wisdom gained.

This doesn't need to be polished. Your focus is on getting the full emotional and intellectual arc on to the page. Use your metaphor, dialogue, or other techniques that felt helpful in earlier exercises.

7: Integration and Care

After completing this intensive emotional work, spend time caring for yourself:

- Write about how it felt to explore this loss creatively.
- Note any insights or surprises that emerged.
- Identify what you need right now (rest, movement, connection, solitude).
- Acknowledge the courage it took to do this work.
- Consider whether this piece wants further development or if it's complete for now.

8: Sharing Consideration

Reflect on whether and how you might want to share this writing:

- Is this piece primarily for your own processing or might it help others?
- What would need to change to make it ready for sharing?
- Who might benefit from reading about your experience?
- What boundaries do you want around sharing this vulnerable work?

Remember: writing about loss isn't about 'getting over it' or finding neat resolutions. It's about finding language for experiences that often feel beyond words and discovering that our deepest wounds can become sources of wisdom and connection. Your pain, transformed through art, becomes a gift you can offer to others walking similar paths.

REIMAGINING YOUR STORY

> 'For decades, I told myself the same story: I was the responsible one, the one who put everyone else first, the one who didn't have time for creative pursuits. It was a true story, but it wasn't the only story. When I started writing at fifty-eight, I discovered other versions of myself—the dreamer who had been waiting patiently, the risk-taker who had been carefully contained, the artist who had been expressing herself in small, unnoticed ways all along. I didn't become a different person when I started writing. I just finally told a fuller story about who I had always been.'
>
> – Maria

The stories we tell about our lives shape not only how we understand our past but also what we believe is possible for our future. Many of us have settled into familiar narratives about who we are, what we're capable of, and what our lives mean. These stories may have served important purposes in helping us make sense of difficult experiences, maintaining consistency in our identity, or protecting us from disappointment. But some of these narratives may have outlived their usefulness. The story that helped you survive your twenties might be limiting you now. The identity that protected you during challenging decades might now be constraining the person you're becoming. Writing offers a unique opportunity to examine these inherited and constructed stories, to challenge the ones that no longer serve you, and to imagine new possibilities for the chapters still to be written.

We all carry stories about ourselves that feel as solid as facts but are actually interpretations and just one possible way of understanding our experiences. These narratives become limiting when they close off possibilities, when they reduce our complexity to simple explanations, or when they trap us in roles that no longer fit who we're becoming.

Limiting narratives often masquerade as objective truths.

- *I'm not creative.*
- *I'm terrible with money.*
- *I always put others first.*
- *I'm not the kind of person who takes risks.*

These statements feel factual because they're supported by evidence, by years of behaviour that seems to confirm them. But they're interpretations of patterns, not immutable laws.

The first step in challenging limiting narratives is recognising them as stories rather than facts. This doesn't mean they're false; your behaviour patterns are real. It means they're just one way of interpreting those patterns.

Many of our most persistent limiting narratives originated in our families of origin. You might have been labelled 'the practical one' while your sibling was 'the creative one', or identified as 'the good girl' in contrast to a 'rebellious' brother. These early role assignments can become so deeply internalised that we continue living them decades after they ceased to be relevant or accurate.

Family narratives also include unspoken rules about what's possible or appropriate:

- People like us don't …
- Women in our family always …

These inherited stories can be particularly powerful because they feel like loyalty to family values rather than limitations on personal possibility.

Beyond family narratives, we inherit stories from our broader culture and generation. Women who came of age in certain eras absorbed messages about appropriate roles, career limitations, the selfishness of creative pursuits, or the incompatibility of motherhood and artistic ambition. While society has changed, these internalised messages can persist long after the external barriers have shifted. Generational stories might include beliefs about ageing: *After fifty, you should focus on grandchildren, not new careers*; about creativity: *Real artists start young;* or about change: *At my age, I shouldn't be trying new things.*

Difficult experiences often generate protective stories that served crucial survival functions but may now be constraining growth. A narrative like *I can't trust people* might have protected you during a dangerous relationship but now prevents healthy connections. *I'm not leadership material* might have kept you safe in a toxic workplace but now limits your confidence in pursuing meaningful opportunities. These protective narratives deserve respect because they helped you survive. But they also deserve examination: are they still serving you, or are they now limiting you?

Limiting narratives are rooted in scarcity thinking: there isn't enough time, opportunity, talent, or permission to go around. These stories might sound like:

- *I've missed my chance.*
- *Other people are more deserving.*
- *There's no point starting now.*
- *Someone my age shouldn't want more.*

Scarcity narratives are particularly insidious because they're often culturally reinforced, especially for women and older adults. But abundance thinking offers an alternative: there's room for your story, your creativity, your late-blooming dreams alongside everyone else's.

Writing offers a unique opportunity to revisit past

experiences and experiment with different ways of understanding them. This isn't about rewriting history or denying difficult realities; it's about recognising that every experience contains multiple possible meanings and choosing interpretations that serve your growth rather than limit it.

Every significant experience in your life can be told from multiple perspectives. The divorce that represents failure from one angle might represent courage and self-advocacy from another. The career interruption for childrearing that feels like a professional setback in one story becomes valuable life experience and skill development in another.

Practice writing the same experience from different narrative perspectives:

- The victim story (what happened to you)
- The hero story (how you responded and grew)
- The learning story (what the experience taught you)
- The connection story (how it helped you understand others)
- The preparation story (how it prepared you for future challenges or opportunities).

None of these versions are truer than others; they're just different lenses that reveal different aspects of your experience. Many limiting narratives cast us as passive recipients of life rather than active agents in our own stories. Reframing often involves identifying moments of choice, resistance, creativity or strength that the original narrative overlooked.

For example, instead of *I wasted twenty years in a job I hated*, you might explore *I chose financial security over immediate satisfaction to provide for my family, and I found ways to maintain my integrity and help others even within constraints I didn't choose.* This reframe doesn't deny the difficulty but recognises the agency and values that guided your choices.

Sometimes limiting narratives focus on surface events while missing deeper themes that run through your life. You might tell a story about career disappointments that overlooks a consistent theme of helping others or focus on relationship failures while missing a pattern of increasing self-awareness and boundary-setting. Look for themes that transcend specific events: resilience, creativity, service, growth, connection, authenticity. These deeper patterns often reveal strengths and consistencies that superficial narratives miss.

One of the most powerful reframes involves seeing past experiences as preparation for your current opportunities. The years you spent managing others' needs developed skills in understanding human motivation that now inform your character development. The loss that devastated you opened capacities for empathy that enrich your writing. The career that felt like a detour provided knowledge and credibility that support your current work.

This isn't about grateful acceptance of suffering; it's about recognising that nothing in your life has been wasted if you can transform it into wisdom, skill, or creative material.

Creating New Possibilities Through Creative Exploration

Once you've identified limiting narratives and experimented with reframing past experiences, writing becomes a laboratory for imagining new possibilities. Creative exploration allows you to try on different versions of yourself, to explore roads not taken, and to envision futures that your old stories might have made unthinkable.

Creative writing thrives on 'what-if' questions, and these can be powerful tools for personal exploration as well as fiction. What if you had made different choices at key moments? What if you prioritised your creative development instead of others' needs? What if you believed you deserved the same opportunities you encourage others to pursue?

These explorations are about expanding your sense of possibility. By imagining alternative versions of your past, you can identify desires, values and capacities that your actual choices may have obscured but didn't eliminate.

Write letters from your future self: the seventy-year-old you, the eighty-year-old you, looking back on the creative risks you took in your fifties and sixties. What does that future self wish you had tried? What does she want you to know about the possibilities that are available to you now?

Creating fictional characters who share some of your circumstances but make different choices can be a safe way to explore alternative possibilities. What would a character based on you do if she believed fully in her creative abilities?

How would she handle the challenges you're facing if she weren't constrained by your limiting narratives?

This technique allows you to explore possibilities through the safety of fiction while potentially discovering insights that apply to your actual life.

Different writing genres offer diverse ways of understanding experience and possibility. Memoir focuses on what happened, but fiction allows you to explore what might happen. Poetry distills experience to its emotional essence. Essays examine ideas and their implications. Experimenting with genres for exploring the same material can reveal different aspects of your experience and different possibilities for understanding and growth.

Sometimes our individual imaginations are constrained by the same limiting beliefs that created our restrictive narratives. Engaging with other writers, joining creative communities, or working with writing mentors can expose you to possibilities you might not generate alone.

Listen to how others talk about their creative journeys, their late-in-life reinventions, their discoveries of hidden talents. Their stories can expand your sense of what's possible for your own story.

Writing Exercise

This exercise will guide you through identifying limiting narratives, reframing key experiences, and exploring new possibilities for your life story.

1: Narrative Archaeology

Identifying core narratives

Complete these sentences as quickly as possible, without editing:

- I am the type of person who always …
- I am not the type of person who …
- People like me don't usually …
- In my family, I was always …
- I've never been good at …
- I'm too old to …
- It's too late for me to …
- I missed my chance to …
- I'm not qualified to … because …

- Real [writers/artists/creative people] are ...

Source investigation: choose the three most limiting statements from above.

For each one, explore:

- Where did this belief come from? (family, culture, specific experiences)
- Who first told you this or when did you first believe it?
- What evidence supports this belief?
- What evidence might contradict it?
- How has this belief shaped your choices?

2: Experience Reframing Workshop

Choose a pivotal experience: select a significant experience from your past that you've typically viewed negatively or as a limitation—a career setback, relationship ending, missed opportunity, family responsibility that derailed plans, health challenge, and so on.

Multiple perspective writing: write about this same experience from five different angles:

1. The victim story: what happened to you, what you lost, how unfair it was

2. The hero story: how you responded, what strength you showed, what you accomplished despite difficulty

3. The learning story: what skills, insights or wisdom you gained from this experience

4. The service story: how this experience equipped you to help or understand others

5. The preparation story: how this experience prepared you for opportunities or challenges that came later.

Notice which perspective feels most familiar and which feels most surprising.

3: Alternative History Creation

Road not taken exploration: choose a major life decision from your past where you had multiple options. Write about what your life might have looked like if you had chosen differently. Focus not on whether the alternative would have been better, but on what different aspects of your personality and potential it might have developed.

Value identification: what do you notice about the values and priorities that guided your actual choice versus the imagined alternative? Are these same values still important to you now, or have your priorities shifted?

4: Future Possibility Visioning

Future self letter: write a letter from your eighty-year-old self to your current self. This future you has lived a creatively fulfilling life and wants to encourage you about what's possible. What does she want you to know? What opportunities does she see that you might be missing? What limiting beliefs does she want you to release?

Possibility brainstorming: if you could release all your limiting narratives, what would you want to try, create or become? Don't worry about practicality; just explore desire and possibility. List at least twenty things, including some that feel completely unrealistic.

5: Character Development

Create a fictional character who shares your basic circumstances (age, family situation, background) but operates from a completely different mindset regarding what's possible.

Character profile:

- What does she believe about creativity, ageing, second chances?
- What risks is she willing to take that you haven't been?

- How does she handle criticism, failure or judgement?
- What does she prioritise that you've been reluctant to prioritise?

Character in action: write a scene where this character faces a creative or life decision like one you're currently facing. How does she approach it differently than you would?

6: New Narrative Construction

Core story rewrite: using insights from the previous exercises, write a new core narrative about yourself. This should include:

- Your key strengths and values (not just roles you've played)
- How your experiences have prepared you for current opportunities
- What's possible for your future that you might not have considered before
- How your limiting beliefs might actually be outdated protective mechanisms.

Integration manifesto: write a brief manifesto about the story you want to live now. Begin with: *I am writing a new chapter of my life story, one where I …*

7: Practical Application

Belief–behaviour gap analysis: compare your new narrative with your current behaviour:

- What actions would someone who believed this new story take?
- Where are you already living in alignment with this new narrative?
- What specific changes would help you embody this new story more fully?

Next chapter planning: identify one specific action you can take this week that aligns with your new narrative rather than your old limiting story. This might be:

- Starting a creative project
- Sharing your work with someone
- Taking a class or joining a group
- Setting a boundary that honours your creative needs
- Applying for an opportunity you would have previously dismissed.

8: Story Sustainability

Obstacle anticipation: what circumstances or relationships might pull you back into old limiting narratives? How will you recognise when this is happening?

Who in your life supports your new narrative? How can you increase exposure to people and influences that reinforce your expanded sense of possibility?

How will you remind yourself of your new story when old limiting beliefs resurface? (Daily reading of your manifesto, weekly review of your reframing exercises, regular check-ins with supportive friends, etc.)

Remember: you are not limited to the stories that brought you this far. Those narratives served important purposes, but you have the power to consciously choose which stories to carry forward and which to release. Your life is not a closed book; it's an ongoing story with many chapters still to be written.

WRITING THE WISDOM YEARS

> 'At sixty-five, I finally understood the difference between information and wisdom. Information is what happened to me—the facts, the events, the chronology of my life. Wisdom is what I've learned from what happened to me—the patterns I recognise, the truths I've discovered, the hard-won insights I want to pass on. When I write from wisdom rather than just experience, my words carry weight they never had before. They resonate not just because they're true to my life,
> but because they're true to life itself.'
>
> – Eleanor

The wisdom years are not simply the accumulation of more experiences; they represent a qualitative shift in how we understand and interpret those experiences. By now, you've lived through enough cycles of loss and renewal, challenge and growth, mistake and learning to recognise patterns that younger people can only theorise about. You've witnessed how stories unfold over decades, how seemingly small choices compound into major life directions, how resilience develops through repeated testing.

This accumulated wisdom is one of your greatest assets as a writer. While younger writers may have technical skill and fresh perspectives, you have something irreplaceable: the authority that comes from having lived. Your job is not just to record what happened to you, but to distil from your experiences the universal truths that can guide, comfort and inspire others navigating similar territories.

The challenge of writing from wisdom is transforming personal experience into universal insight without sacrificing specificity or authenticity. Raw experience, no matter how dramatic, doesn't automatically translate into powerful writing. It's the reflection, analysis and meaning-making that transform experience into wisdom, and wisdom into art.

New writers often focus primarily on events: what happened, when it happened, who was involved. Wisdom writing goes deeper, exploring the significance behind the events. Instead of just describing your divorce, you explore what the experience taught you about commitment, compromise, personal growth, or the evolution of love. Instead of simply recounting your career change, you examine what you learned about courage, identity, societal expectations, or the relationship between security and fulfilment.

This shift from event-focused to meaning-focused writing requires patience and reflection. You need to live with an experience long enough to understand its deeper implications, to see how it connects to larger patterns in your life, and to recognise what wisdom it contains that might be valuable to others.

Fresh experiences often carry too much emotional charge

to be transformed into wisdom writing. Time doesn't just heal wounds—it also provides perspective that allows you to see experiences more clearly. The parenting challenges that felt overwhelming in the moment may, with distance, reveal insights about unconditional love, letting go, or the courage required to raise independent human beings.

This is why we writers have a particular advantage: you've had time for experiences to settle, for emotions to integrate, for patterns to become visible. The wisdom you write from has been tested by time and confirmed by reflection.

Be aware that there is a difference between sharing wisdom and delivering lectures. Wisdom writing shows rather than tells, invites rather than insists, explores rather than declares. Instead of writing 'You should never stay in a relationship that doesn't honour your authentic self', you might explore the specific moments when you realised you had been hiding parts of yourself, the fear and courage involved in becoming more authentic, and the unexpected ways relationships changed when you did. Trust that your readers will extract their own lessons from your carefully rendered experience. Your job is to be honest about your journey; their job is to figure out what applies to theirs.

Counterintuitively, the more specific and personal your writing, the more universal it becomes. Generic advice about 'following your dreams' resonates less than the specific story of how you left a secure job at fifty-two to start a pottery studio, including the sleepless nights, the financial fears, the awkward conversations with concerned relatives, and the moment you realised you were finally living as yourself.

Specificity creates credibility and emotional connection. Readers don't just understand your wisdom intellectually—they feel it through the specific details of your experience.

Our lives naturally bring philosophical questioning as we grapple with mortality, meaning, legacy, and the larger patterns of existence. These philosophical explorations will add depth and resonance to your writing, whether you're writing memoir, fiction, poetry or essays.

Certain philosophical questions become more pressing with age and experience. What does it mean to live a meaningful life? How do we find purpose in the face of uncertainty and loss? What do we owe to future generations? How do we balance acceptance with the desire for continued growth? What is the relationship between individual fulfilment and service to others? These aren't abstract academic questions when you're living them; they're urgent personal inquiries that arise from real experience. Your writing can explore these questions not through theoretical analysis but through the lived experience that gives them weight and meaning.

Your life has been a decades-long experiment in being human. Every major decision, relationship, loss and discovery has provided data about how life works, what matters, and what endures. This experiential knowledge gives you unique insights into philosophical questions that younger people can only approach theoretically.

For example, your experience of caring for ageing parents provides firsthand knowledge about dignity, interdependence, the cycle of generations, and what it means to love someone through decline. Your experience of watching children become adults offers insights into autonomy, influence, legacy, and letting go. Your experience of career transitions illuminates questions about identity, purpose, security, and what constitutes success.

A hallmark of wisdom is the ability to hold contradictions without rushing to resolve them. You may have learned that people can be simultaneously selfish and generous, that love can coexist with frustration, that endings can be both devastating and liberating. This comfort with complexity allows you to write about philosophical questions in nuanced ways that reflect the actual messiness of human experience.

When you explore philosophical questions through your writing, you're not just processing your own experience—you're providing companionship for others grappling with similar questions. Your honest exploration of meaning, mortality, purpose and connection can help readers feel less alone in their own philosophical wrestling. Allow this sense of service to guide your philosophical writing towards humility and connection rather than dogmatism or self-importance. You're not writing as an expert who has figured everything out, but as a fellow traveller sharing insights from the journey.

The art of wisdom writing lies in recognising which aspects of your personal experience connect to universal human themes and then rendering those connections in ways that feel both authentic to your specific story and relevant to readers with completely different circumstances. Universal themes are the fundamental experiences and challenges that characterise human existence across cultures, generations and circumstances. These include love and loss, growth and stagnation, connection and isolation, meaning and meaninglessness, freedom and responsibility, hope and despair, acceptance and change.

Every personal experience holds multiple universal themes. The story of your mother's death might explore themes of generational love, mortality, caregiving, grief, family dynamics, and the ways we honour those who shaped us. Your experience of starting a business might illuminate themes of risk and security, creativity and pragmatism, independence and collaboration, or the relationship between personal fulfilment and financial responsibility.

Learning to identify these universal themes in your individual experiences allows you to write in ways that transcend the specifics of your particular circumstances while remaining grounded in authentic detail. Effective wisdom writing moves fluidly between the deeply personal and the broadly universal. You zoom in to provide specific, authentic details that make your experience vivid and credible. Then you zoom out to explore how those specific details illuminate larger truths about human experience.

For example, you might zoom in to describe the exact moment you decided to end your marriage: the conversation, the setting, the physical sensations of that realisation. Then you zoom out to explore what this decision revealed about the evolution of relationships, the courage required for difficult choices, or the ways we grow beyond the people we once were.

Your specific cultural, generational and social context is part of what makes your experience unique and valuable.

But wisdom writing also builds bridges between different contexts, showing how fundamental human experiences transcend cultural boundaries.

You might write about the particular challenges of being a woman in your generation and industry, while also exploring universal themes of ambition, discrimination, persistence, and the evolution of social expectations. Your specific context provides authenticity and detail; the universal themes provide relevance and connection.

The most effective wisdom writing invites readers to find their own experiences reflected in yours, even when the surface details are completely different. A reader who has never experienced divorce might still connect deeply with your exploration of how identity shifts when major relationships end. Someone from a different cultural background might recognise their own struggles with family expectations in your story about career choices.

This co-creation happens when you write with enough specificity to be credible and enough universality to be relatable, when you explore the emotional and philosophical dimensions of experience rather than just the factual ones.

Writing Exercise

This exercise will help you identify the wisdom embedded in your experiences and transform it into writing that connects your personal insights to universal human themes.

1: Life Lesson Inventory

Make a list of significant experiences from your life, organised by category:

- Major relationships (marriage, divorce, parenting, friendship, loss)
- Career and work experiences (successes, failures, transitions, discoveries)
- Health and ageing experiences (illness, recovery, physical changes, vitality)
- Family dynamics (caring for parents, sibling relationships, generational patterns)
- Personal growth moments (overcoming fears, developing skills, changing beliefs)
- Loss and grief experiences (deaths, endings, disappointments, letting go).

For each category, identify two to three specific experiences that feel significant to your development.

Choose three experiences from your list. For each one, complete these prompts:

- What I learned about myself from this experience was …
- What I learned about relationships/life/human nature was …
- What I wish I had known beforehand was …
- What I would tell someone facing something similar is …

2: Philosophical Question Exploration

Based on your life experiences, write your current thoughts on these philosophical questions:

- What does it mean to live a meaningful life?
- How do we balance self-care with care for others?
- What is the relationship between security and growth?
- How do we find purpose in the face of uncertainty?
- What do we owe to future generations?
- How do we love people while accepting their limitations?

- What is the role of suffering in human development?

Choose the question that feels most urgent or interesting to you.

Identify specific experiences from your life that have shaped your thinking about your chosen philosophical question. How has lived experience informed your perspective in ways that pure thinking could not?

3: Universal Theme Mapping

Choose one significant experience from 1. Map the universal themes it contains:

Surface level (what happened):

- Basic facts of the experience
- When and where it occurred
- Who was involved?

Emotional level (how it felt):

- Primary emotions you experienced
- How these emotions evolved over time
- Unexpected feelings that emerged.

Philosophical level (what it means):

- What this experience revealed about human nature
- How it changed your understanding of life
- What universal truths it illuminated.

Universal themes (how others might connect):

- What fundamental human experiences does this story illustrate?
- How might someone with a completely different background still relate to your experience?
- What aspects transcend your specific circumstances?

From your universal themes, choose the one that feels most important to explore in your writing.

4: Wisdom Writing Practice

Write about your chosen experience, moving from specific personal details to universal insights. Structure your writing this way:

- Opening: start with a specific, vivid scene from your experience. Use concrete details to place the reader in the moment with you.

- Explore what this experience taught you, how it changed you, what you discovered about yourself or life. Move between specific details and broader insights.
- Explore how your specific experience illuminates universal human themes. What might others facing different but related challenges learn from your journey?

End your piece with a wisdom statement, not a preachy lesson, but a hard-won insight that emerges naturally from your experience. This should feel earned by the story you've told.

5: Philosophical Integration

Rewrite a portion of your piece from 4, but this time let your philosophical exploration emerge through narrative and reflection rather than direct statement. Instead of saying 'I learned that …,' show the reader the moment of realisation, the gradual shift in understanding, or the behaviour change that demonstrated new wisdom.

End with a question rather than an answer, something your experience opened up rather than closed down. What questions does your story raise for readers to consider in their own lives?

6: Reader Connection Assessment

Review your writing and assess:

- What details are specific to your circumstances vs universally relatable?
- Where might readers with different backgrounds still find connection?
- What emotions or insights transcend your particular situation?
- How could someone facing a completely different challenge still find wisdom in your story?

Identify one place in your writing where you could strengthen the bridge between your specific experience and universal themes. Revise that section to make the connection more explicit without becoming preachy.

7: Wisdom Series Planning

Based on this exercise, identify other experiences and philosophical questions you want to explore in your writing:

- What other life lessons deserve deeper exploration?
- Which philosophical questions feel most urgent to examine?

- How might you create a series of pieces that explore related themes?
- What wisdom do you most want to share with others?

Complete this statement: 'Through my wisdom writing, I want to offer others …'

8: Revision and Refinement

Review your piece and identify any places where you might be lecturing rather than sharing. Ensure that your wisdom statements emerge authentically from your experience rather than from what you think you should have learned. Wisdom writing must be honest about the messiness and complexity of real learning.

Remember: your wisdom is not just personal achievement; it's a gift you can offer to others navigating the complexities of being human. The insights you've gained through decades of living, reflecting and growing have value beyond your own understanding. When you write from wisdom, you're not just telling your story; you're offering companionship and guidance to others on the human journey.

LEGACY ON THE PAGE

'When my granddaughter was born, I suddenly understood why I needed to write my stories down. Not because they were extraordinary, but because they were ordinary—and therefore in danger of being forgotten. I realised that in fifty years, she might wonder what her great-grandmother was really like, what I worried about, what made me laugh, how I navigated the challenges of my time. My writing isn't just creative expression anymore; it's a bridge across generations, a way of saying I was here, I mattered, and you came from something rich and complex and fully human.'

– Patricia

The desire to leave something meaningful behind often intensifies in midlife, particularly for women who have spent decades nurturing others and may wonder what lasting impact they've made beyond their immediate family circle. Writing offers a unique form of legacy, one that preserves not just facts and events, but voice, personality, wisdom, and the particular way you've experienced being human in your specific time and place.

But legacy writing raises complex questions that go beyond craft and creativity. When you write about your life, you're inevitably writing about other people's lives too. When you share family stories, you're making private experiences public. When you offer your perspective on events that others experienced differently, you're claiming authority over shared narrative territory. Navigating these ethical complexities while honouring your authentic voice and important stories requires both courage and careful consideration.

Writing for future generations requires a different mindset than writing for contemporary audiences. You're addressing people you may never meet, who will inherit a world you can only imagine, who may find your historical moment as distant and strange as you find your grandparents' era. This long view can be both liberating and daunting. Future generations will inherit the outcomes of decisions made in your lifetime, but they may lack an understanding of the context in which those decisions were made. Your writing can provide invaluable historical and emotional context that helps them understand not just what happened, but why it happened and how it felt to live through it.

Consider the major events, cultural shifts, and social movements of your lifetime. Future readers may know the historical facts, but your personal account can illuminate what it felt like to live through the women's liberation movement, the digital revolution, economic recessions, cultural changes, or global events. Your perspective as someone who experienced these changes firsthand has historical value beyond its personal significance.

Historical records capture major events, but the texture of daily life—how people actually lived, what they worried about, what brought them joy—often disappears unless someone takes care to preserve it. Your writing can capture the details that give future generations a sense of what ordinary life was like in your era.

- What did your house smell like?
- What were your daily routines?
- What technology seemed miraculous when it first appeared?
- What social conventions seem strange in retrospect?
- What were you afraid of that turned out to be nothing?
- What did you worry was temporary that turned out to be permanent?

These details create a rich portrait of lived experience that historical texts rarely capture.

Beyond events and daily life, your writing can transmit values, wisdom, and hard-won insights to people who will face different challenges but similar fundamental human dilemmas. The specific circumstances of their lives may be unimaginable to you, but the core questions—how to love well, how to find meaning, how to handle loss, how to make difficult decisions—remain constant.

Your legacy writing can explore not just what you believed, but how you came to believe it, how your values evolved through experience, and what you learned about living according to principles under pressure. This kind of values transmission is often more powerful than direct advice because it shows rather than tells. You are the repository of family stories, cultural traditions, and generational knowledge that could disappear if you don't preserve them. Who tells the stories about your parents' courtship, your grandmother's resilience, the family migrations and struggles and triumphs? What cultural traditions, recipes, customs and wisdom have been passed down to you that you could pass forward through writing? These stories don't have to be dramatic to be valuable. Sometimes the most treasured family stories are about ordinary moments that capture personality, relationships, or the flavour of a particular time and place.

Writing about family presents unique ethical challenges because it involves people who didn't choose to be characters in your story but who may be significantly affected by how you portray them. Balancing honesty with kindness, authenticity with respect, and your right to tell your story with others' rights to privacy requires careful thought and sometimes difficult choices.

Ideally, you would have consent from everyone you write about, but this is often impractical or impossible. Some family members may be deceased, estranged, or unwilling to take part in your writing project. Some may want veto power over how they're portrayed, which could compromise your authentic voice and honest perspective. There's no perfect solution to this dilemma, but there are principles that can guide your decisions. Consider the difference between writing about people versus writing about your experience of people. You can honestly describe how someone's behaviour affected you without claiming to know their motivations or inner life. You can share your perspective on family dynamics without insisting that yours is the only valid viewpoint.

Some family members deserve extra protection in your writing: children, people with mental illness, those struggling with addiction, or anyone whose privacy could be significantly violated by your revelations. Consider whether sharing certain stories serves any purpose beyond satisfying your desire for complete honesty. This doesn't mean avoiding difficult topics, but it does mean being thoughtful about how you approach them. You might focus on your own experience of dealing with a family member's addiction rather than providing detailed accounts of their behaviour. You might write about the impact of mental illness on family dynamics without exposing personal details about the affected individual.

Your truth—how you experienced events, what they meant to you, how they affected you—is valid and important. But it's different from claiming factual authority over events that others may remember differently. Acknowledging this difference in your writing can help you tell your truth without invalidating others' experiences. Phrases like 'as I remember it,' 'from my perspective,' or 'the way I experienced it' signal to readers that you're sharing your subjective truth rather than claiming objective authority. This doesn't weaken your narrative; it strengthens it by demonstrating self-awareness and respect for the complexity of family relationships.

Before writing about difficult family situations, examine

your motivations honestly. Are you sharing this story because it's essential to understanding your experience and growth? Does it serve a larger purpose in your narrative or message? Or are you sharing it primarily to vent, get revenge, or prove a point? Revenge memoirs rarely serve anyone well, including their authors. The most powerful family writing often comes from a place of hard-won understanding, forgiveness, or at least acceptance rather than from raw anger or hurt.

Sometimes the most ethical choice is to wait. A story that feels necessary to tell immediately after a family crisis might feel less urgent after time has passed and wounds have healed. Conversely, some stories become more important to tell as you gain distance and perspective.

Consider not just whether you have the right to tell a story, but whether this is the right time to tell it. Will sharing this now help or harm relationships that matter to you? Will you feel differently about this story in five or ten years?

The ultimate goal of legacy writing isn't just preservation; it's connection. Your stories become truly meaningful when they serve others, when they help people feel less alone, when they provide guidance or comfort or inspiration to those who need it. When you share your authentic experiences, especially difficult ones, you give others permission to acknowledge and explore their own similar experiences. Your story about struggling with depression might help someone feel less ashamed of their mental health challenges. Your account of caring for ageing parents might provide practical and emotional guidance to someone facing similar responsibilities. This ripple effect extends beyond your immediate audience. Your writing might influence one person who then shares their story, which influences someone else, creating connections and understanding that extend far beyond your original words.

Many families carry unspoken stories, traumas, secrets, patterns of behaviour that everyone knows about but no one discusses. Your willingness to write honestly about these experiences can break destructive patterns of silence and shame. This doesn't mean exposing every family secret or airing all grievances publicly. But it might mean being the first person to write honestly about depression in your family, or about the impact of immigration, or about patterns of dysfunction that have affected multiple generations. Your courage to speak can create space for others to speak too.

In a culture that often demands we present polished, perfect versions of ourselves, authentic writing about real struggles and genuine growth provides a valuable counternarrative. Your willingness to be honest about your mistakes, uncertainties, and ongoing growth can inspire others to embrace their own imperfections and continue developing. This is particularly important for women, who often feel pressure to appear to have everything figured out. Your honest account of your journey, including the detours, mistakes, and ongoing discoveries can help other women feel permission to be authentic about their own experiences.

Your individual story contributes to our collective understanding of what it means to be human in your particular time and circumstances. Women's stories, especially, have often been underrepresented in historical records and literary culture. Your voice adds to the growing chorus of women's experiences being preserved and honoured. Finding purpose in your painful experiences can be an important part of healing. The losses, mistakes and struggles that once felt meaningless can gain significance when they become part of a story that helps others. This doesn't minimise the original pain, but it can transform it into something valuable.

The mother who writes about losing a child might help other grieving parents feel less alone. The woman who writes about rebuilding her life after divorce might inspire others to find courage for necessary changes. The person who writes about overcoming addiction might provide hope to those still struggling.

Writing Exercise

This exercise will help you explore what stories you want to preserve for future generations while navigating the ethical considerations of family writing and discovering the purpose your stories might serve.

1: Legacy Intention Setting

Imagine someone reading your writing fifty years from now, perhaps a descendant you'll never meet, or a stranger who finds your work meaningful. Write a letter to this future reader explaining:

- What you want them to know about you as a person (beyond your roles and achievements)
- What you want them to understand about your historical moment
- What wisdom or insights you hope to share that might be relevant to their life
- What values or principles you hope to pass forward.

Legacy goals clarification: complete these statements:

- Through my writing, I want to preserve …
- I want future generations to understand that …
- The most important thing I've learned that I want to share is …
- If my writing could prevent future generations from making one mistake, it would be …
- If my writing could help someone feel less alone, it would be about …

2: Story Inventory and Ethical Assessment

Create categories and list significant family stories you might want to write about:

- Stories of resilience: how family members overcame challenges, adapted to change, survived difficult times
- Cultural heritage: traditions, customs, immigration stories, cultural identity, generational changes
- Relationship dynamics: love stories, family conflicts, generational patterns, communication styles
- Difficult experiences: trauma, addiction, mental illness, loss, family secrets or dysfunction
- Daily life details: how your family lived, what was

normal in your household, unique family customs or quirks
- Personal growth: how family experiences shaped your development, values you inherited or rejected.

Ethical assessment: for the more sensitive stories on your list, consider:

- Who could be hurt by this story being public?
- What is my motivation for telling this story?
- Is this essential to my larger narrative, or peripheral?
- How might I tell my truth without violating others' privacy?
- Should I wait longer before sharing this story?
- Could I focus on my experience rather than others' behaviour?

3: Historical and Cultural Context Writing

Choose a decade from your life and write about what it was like to live through that time:

- What major events shaped that period?
- What was daily life like in ways that might seem strange to future generations?

- What did people worry about? Hope for? Take for granted?
- What technology, social customs, or cultural norms have changed significantly since then?
- What was it like to be a woman of your age and circumstances during that time?

Add to your description: how has your perspective on that era changed with time?

- What seemed important then that feels less significant now?
- What seemed minor then that you now recognise as historically significant?

4: Values and Wisdom Transmission

Identify three to five values that are central to who you are. For each value, write about:

- A specific experience that taught you this value's importance
- How this value has guided difficult decisions
- How your understanding of this value has evolved over time
- What you want future generations to understand about living according to this principle.

Write letters to imaginary people facing challenges you've navigated:

- To a young woman starting her career
- To someone caring for ageing parents
- To a person facing a major loss
- To someone questioning their life choices
- To a woman wondering if it's too late to pursue her dreams.

Focus on sharing insight rather than advice, understanding rather than answers.

5: Purpose-Driven Story Selection

From your story inventory, identify which stories might serve specific purposes:

- Which stories might help others feel less alone in their struggles?
- Which stories illustrate important values or life lessons?
- Which stories preserve important family or cultural history?
- Which stories challenge harmful stereotypes or social expectations?

- Which stories model resilience, growth, or positive change?

Choose one story that you feel called to write not just for personal expression but because it might genuinely help others. Write a brief mission statement for this story:

- *I want to write this story because …*

6: Ethical Writing Strategy

Develop ethical guidelines when telling family stories:

- How will you focus on your experience rather than making claims about others' motivations?
- What details are essential vs what could be changed or omitted to protect privacy?
- How will you acknowledge that your perspective is one of many?
- What stories will you wait to tell until more time has passed?
- How might you seek input from family members without giving them veto power?

Truth and respect balance: write a personal ethics statement for your family writing:

- *When I write about family, I commit to …*

Include principles about honesty, respect, timing and purpose.

7: Legacy Project Planning

Based on this exercise, define a specific legacy writing project:

- What format will serve your goals best? (memoir, family history, essay collection, letters to descendants)
- What stories are essential to include?
- What themes or values do you want to emphasise?
- Who is your primary audience? (family, broader public, specific demographics)
- What ethical boundaries will guide your writing?

Identification:

- What's the first story you want to write for this project?
- What research or reflection do you need to do first?
- What conversations (if any) do you want to have with family members?
- How will you balance authenticity with responsibility to others?

8: Future Connection

Write a scene imagining someone in the future reading your legacy writing. Who are they? What do they take from your words? How do your stories affect them? What do they understand about you, your era, or human experience that they wouldn't have known otherwise?

This visualisation can help clarify the deeper purpose of your legacy writing and motivate you through the challenging work of ethical family storytelling.

Remember: your stories matter not because your life was extraordinary, but because it was authentically lived and thoughtfully examined. The ordinary details of how you navigated love, loss, growth and change provide invaluable guidance and connection for those who come after you. Your legacy isn't just what you accomplished—it's what you understood, how you grew, and what wisdom you can pass forward.

CREATING SUSTAINABLE WRITING RHYTHMS

'For years, I tried to write like I was twenty-five—pulling all-nighters, waiting for inspiration to strike, writing in intense bursts followed by long periods of nothing. It never worked, and I always felt like I was failing as a writer. When I finally accepted that I needed a different approach at fifty-four, everything changed. I started writing for thirty minutes every morning before anyone else woke up. No drama, no waiting for perfect conditions, just consistent showing up. Three years later, I've completed two novels and a memoir. The secret wasn't more time or more talent—it was finding a rhythm that actually worked with my life instead of against it.'

– Linda

Sustainability is the secret weapon of any writer. Creating a sustainable writing practice means designing a rhythm that honours both your creative needs and your life's realities, a practice that can weather illness, family crises, busy seasons, and the natural ebbs and flows of creative energy. A sustainable writing practice isn't about finding more time; it's about using the time you have more intentionally. It's not about writing faster or longer; it's about writing more consistently. It's not about eliminating all obstacles; it's about building a practice resilient enough to survive them.

The biggest mistake writers make is trying to force their lives to accommodate an idealised writing practice rather than designing a practice that fits their actual circumstances. Your writing practice needs to work with your energy patterns, family responsibilities, health considerations, and seasonal rhythms—not in spite of them.

Before you can design a sustainable practice, you need to honestly assess how much time you actually have available for writing, not how much you wish you had. Track your time for a week, noting not just when you're busy, but when you're mentally and physically available for creative work. Consider the difference between clock time and quality time. You might have two hours available, but only forty minutes of peak mental energy. Better to plan for forty minutes of focused writing than two hours of distracted struggle. Quality trumps quantity every time, especially when you're building a long-term practice.

Your creative energy doesn't distribute evenly throughout the day or week. Some people are naturally most creative in the early morning; others find their flow in the evening. Some days of the week feel more conducive to writing than others. Sometimes of the month or seasons of the year affect your creative availability. Track your energy patterns for a few weeks. When do you feel most mentally alert? When do ideas flow most easily? When does your inner critic seem quieter? Design your writing practice around these natural rhythms rather than fighting against them.

When time is limited, micro-practices can be surprisingly powerful. Writing for fifteen minutes daily often produces more consistent progress than waiting for two-hour blocks that rarely materialise. These brief sessions also train your brain to shift into creative mode quickly—a valuable skill for busy people.

Consider these micro-practices:

- Morning pages: 15 minutes of stream-of-consciousness writing to clear mental clutter
- Lunch break writing: 20 to 30 minutes of focused creative work
- Commute composing: using voice memos to capture ideas or draft passages
- Evening reflection: 10 minutes of writing about the day or planning tomorrow's work.

Just as gardens require different care in different seasons, your writing practice may need seasonal adjustments. You might be more productive during winter's quiet months or more creative during spring's energy surge. Holiday seasons might require reduced writing commitments, while vacation periods might offer opportunities for intensive work.

Build flexibility into your practice by identifying your peak writing seasons and planning accordingly. Use high-energy seasons for ambitious projects and lower-energy seasons for maintenance work like editing or organising.

The most sustainable practices attach to routines you're already committed to maintaining. If you already get up early to exercise, consider adding fifteen minutes for writing. If you have a sacred evening tea ritual, incorporate some writing time. If you always take a walk after dinner, bring a notebook for capturing ideas. This integration approach requires less willpower because you're building on existing habits rather than creating entirely new ones. It also reduces the number of decisions you need to make about when and where to write.

Consistency is more powerful than intensity for building a sustainable writing practice. Regular, modest efforts compound over time, creating momentum that carries you through inevitable obstacles and low-motivation periods. Consistency isn't about producing brilliant work every day—it's about showing up to the page regularly, regardless of mood, inspiration or circumstances. Some days you'll write beautifully; other days you'll produce mediocre work; occasionally you'll write complete garbage. All of this is part of the process.

The act of showing up regularly trains your creative mind to be available on demand rather than waiting for perfect conditions. It also builds confidence in your identity as a writer; you become someone who writes regularly, not someone who writes only when inspired.

Set your daily writing commitment at a level you can maintain even on your worst days. Better to commit to ten minutes daily and exceed it regularly than to commit to an hour daily and miss it frequently. You can always write longer when time and energy allow, but having a backup minimum ensures you maintain momentum. This minimum should feel almost ridiculously achievable. If ten minutes feels like too much some days, try five. The goal is to establish the habit of showing up; the volume will increase naturally over time.

Keep simple records of your writing practice to maintain motivation and identify patterns. This doesn't need to be elaborate: a simple calendar where you mark days you wrote, or a notebook where you record daily word counts or time spent writing. Tracking serves multiple purposes: it makes your progress visible (which is motivating), it helps you identify when you're most and least productive, and it provides data for adjusting your practice. When you can see that you've written twenty out of the last thirty days, skipping a day feels less like failure and more like a normal part of a successful practice.

Link your writing practice to an existing strong habit to make it more automatic:

- *After I pour my morning coffee, I write for 15 minutes.*
- *Before I check email, I write for 10 minutes, which creates a clear trigger for your writing practice.*

Choose a trigger that happens every day and that you're unlikely to skip. Morning routines often work well because they're less likely to be disrupted by external demands than evening routines.

Find ways to be accountable to your writing practice without creating pressure that undermines creativity. This might mean joining a writing group that meets regularly, finding a writing partner to check in with weekly, or simply telling a supportive friend about your writing goals. The key is choosing accountability that feels supportive rather than judgemental. You want encouragement to continue, not shame when you stumble.

Creative energy naturally fluctuates, and a sustainable writing practice needs to accommodate these rhythms rather than fight them. Understanding and working with your creative cycles can help you maintain productivity even during low-energy periods. Most writers experience predictable cycles of high creative energy followed by periods of lower productivity. These cycles might correlate with seasons, hormonal fluctuations, life stress, or simply the natural rhythm of creative work: periods of intense output followed by necessary fallow times for replenishment. Learn to recognise your personal cycles without judging them as good or bad. High-energy periods are for creation and ambitious projects; lower-energy periods are for editing, organising, research, or simply maintaining the habit of showing up to the page.

Your writing practice can adapt to different phases of creativity and life circumstances. During high-energy periods, you might write new material, tackle challenging projects, or increase your daily time commitment. During lower-energy periods, you might focus on editing existing work, organising files, reading for inspiration, or maintaining minimal daily writing just to preserve the habit. This flexibility prevents the all-or-nothing thinking that destroys writing practices. Instead of abandoning your practice during difficult periods, you adjust it to fit your current capacity.

Creative resistance is normal and doesn't mean you should stop writing. Sometimes resistance signals that you need to approach your work differently; perhaps the project isn't ready, or you need to research more, or your approach isn't working. Other times resistance is simply the creative mind's version of stage fright. Develop strategies for working with resistance rather than fighting it. This might mean switching to a different project, changing your writing location, trying a different time of day, or simply acknowledging the resistance and writing anyway. Sometimes the best work emerges from writing through resistance rather than waiting for it to disappear.

Just as fields need to lie fallow between plantings to restore nutrients to the soil, creative minds need periods of apparent inactivity to replenish. Reading, observing, living, processing experiences are all part of the creative process even when they don't produce immediate output. Learn to trust these fallow periods rather than judging them as laziness or failure. Use them for input activities: reading, watching films, having conversations, travelling, or simply paying attention to life. Often your next creative breakthrough is gestating during these apparently unproductive periods.

Life inevitably brings periods of crisis, illness, family emergencies, or overwhelming responsibilities that make regular writing impossible. Rather than abandoning your writing practice entirely during these times, find minimal ways to maintain connection to your creative work.

This might mean carrying a notebook to jot down observations, writing a single sentence daily, or simply reading for ten minutes. The goal is to maintain the identity and connection to writing so you can return to more active practice when circumstances allow.

Plan different types of writing projects for different seasons of your creative and personal life. Use high-energy periods for first drafts and creative breakthroughs. Use medium-energy periods for revision and editing. Use low-energy periods for research, organisation, and planning future projects. This ensures you're always making some kind of progress on your writing, even when your energy for creation is low. It also prevents the guilt and frustration that come from expecting constant high-level creative output.

Writing Exercise

This exercise will help you assess your current situation and design a realistic, sustainable writing practice that works with your life rather than against it.

1: Life and Energy Assessment

For one week, track how you actually spend your time in thirty-minute blocks. At the end of the week, identify:

- Periods when you're alone and mentally available
- Times when you feel most alert and creative
- Recurring commitments that can't be moved
- Time currently spent on activities you could reduce or eliminate
- Windows of opportunity you might not have considered (commute time, waiting periods, early mornings, etc.).

Create a daily energy map noting:

- What time of day do you feel most mentally sharp?
- When do you feel most emotionally available for creative work?
- What days of the week tend to be more or less stressful?
- How do seasonal changes affect your energy and mood?
- What activities drain your creative energy vs restore it?

2: Current Practice Evaluation

Reflect on past attempts to establish a writing practice:

- What writing routines have you tried before?
- Which attempts lasted longest and why?
- What obstacles consistently derailed your practice?
- What conditions or circumstances supported your writing best?
- What expectations were unrealistic for your actual life?

Creating Sustainable Writing Rhythms

List current barriers to consistent writing:

- Time constraints and competing priorities
- Physical comfort and workspace issues
- Mental/emotional obstacles (perfectionism, self-doubt, overwhelm)
- External interruptions and demands
- Lack of accountability or support.

3: Sustainable Practice Design

Design a writing practice you could maintain even during your busiest or most challenging weeks:

- How much time can you commit daily without feeling overwhelmed?
- What time of day offers the most consistency?
- Where will you write? (What backup locations if your primary space isn't available?)
- What materials/tools do you need to make writing as easy as possible?
- What would this practice look like on a bad day?

Design an expanded version for when you have more time and energy:

- How would you expand your minimum practice during good periods?
- What additional projects could you tackle during high-energy seasons?
- How might you batch certain activities (research, editing, planning) during appropriate times?

Create guidelines for adapting your practice:

- How will you scale down during difficult periods without abandoning writing entirely?
- How will you recognise when you need to adjust your practice?
- What signals will tell you when you're ready to expand again?

4: Habit Integration Strategy

Identify existing routines where you could attach writing:

- What do you do consistently every day that could serve as a trigger?
- How could you modify your morning or evening routine to include writing?

Creating Sustainable Writing Rhythms

- What transitions in your day (after coffee, before dinner, etc.) could become writing cues?

Plan how to make writing as easy and attractive as possible:

- How will you prepare your writing space?
- What materials will you keep readily available?
- How can you minimise setup time and decision-making?
- What will make writing feel pleasant rather than burdensome?

5: Momentum and Accountability Plan

Design a simple system for tracking your writing practice:

- How will you record your daily writing (calendar marks, word counts, time spent)?
- What metrics matter most to you (consistency, word count, time, projects completed)?
- How often will you review your progress?
- How will you celebrate milestones and consistency streaks?

Identify accountability and encouragement sources:

- Who in your life supports your writing goals?
- What writing communities (online or local) could provide encouragement?
- How might you find a writing partner or accountability buddy?
- What boundaries do you need to protect your writing time?

6: Cycle and Season Planning

Based on your experience, identify your personal patterns:

- What times of year do you feel most/least creative?
- How do life stresses typically affect your writing energy?
- What early warning signs tell you when you're heading into a low-energy period?
- How long do your high-energy and low-energy periods typically last?

Plan different types of writing activities for different energy levels:

- High-energy periods: what ambitious projects will you tackle?

Creating Sustainable Writing Rhythms

- Medium-energy periods: what steady progress work can you do?
- Low-energy periods: what maintenance activities will keep you connected to writing?

7: Implementation Strategy

Rather than trying to implement everything at once, plan a gradual introduction:

- Week 1: what single element will you start with?
- Week 2–4: how will you build on this foundation?
- Month 2: what additional elements will you add?
- What signals will tell you when you're ready to expand?

Anticipate and plan for likely challenges:

- What will you do when you miss several days in a row?
- How will you handle travel or illness?
- What's your plan for busy seasons (holidays, work deadlines, family events)?
- How will you restart if your practice gets completely derailed?

8: Practice Declaration

Write a brief manifesto for your sustainable writing practice:

- *I commit to writing [frequency] for [duration] because …*
- *My writing practice will honour both my creative needs and my life responsibilities by …*
- *When obstacles arise, I will …*
- *I will know my practice is working when …*

Keep this declaration visible as a reminder of your intention and commitment.

Remember: the goal isn't to create the perfect writing practice—it's to create a practice that actually works with your real life and that you can maintain over time. A modest practice you sustain for years will produce far more writing than an ambitious practice you abandon after a few weeks. Start small, be consistent, and trust that sustainable rhythms will carry you much further than sporadic bursts of activity.

BEYOND MEMOIR

'For years, I thought I had to choose between truth and imagination, between my real experiences and made-up stories. Then I realised that the best fiction comes from emotional truth, even when the facts are invented. My decades of living, watching relationships evolve, seeing how people respond to crisis, understanding the small moments that reveal character—these became my greatest assets as a fiction writer. I don't write about what happened to me; I write about what could happen to someone, informed by everything I've learned about how people actually behave.'

– Carol

While memoir and personal narrative feel like natural starting points for some writers, fiction and poetry offer different kinds of creative freedom and expression. These forms allow you to transcend the limitations of your actual experience while drawing deeply from the wisdom and observation skills you've developed over decades of living. You can explore themes and situations that fascinate you without being constrained by what happened. You can give voice to parts of yourself that never had the chance to fully express in real life.

A writer brings unique advantages to imaginative writing: emotional depth, understanding of human complexity, freedom from the need to impress others with cleverness, and the confidence that comes from knowing yourself. You no longer need to prove your intelligence or shock anyone with your daring; you can focus on the deeper work of creating authentic, resonant art.

The best fiction doesn't emerge from pure imagination; it grows from the fertile ground of lived experience, observation, and emotional understanding. Your decades of watching people, navigating relationships, and experiencing life's complexities have given you an invaluable foundation for creating believable characters and authentic fictional worlds.

Fiction writing allows you to separate emotional truth from factual truth in powerful ways. You might never have been divorced, but if you've experienced the end of any significant relationship, you understand the emotional territory of loss, disappointment, relief, and new beginnings. You can use this emotional knowledge to write convincingly about a character's divorce, even if the external circumstances are completely different from anything you've experienced.

This is where you have a significant advantage. You've experienced enough variations on human emotions: love, grief, betrayal, joy, fear, hope and understand their nuances. You know that anger often masks hurt, that relief can accompany loss, that people rarely feel just one thing at a time. This emotional sophistication translates directly into more complex, believable characters.

You've seen how people respond differently to stress, how

they reveal their values through small actions, how they change over time, how they surprise you with their resilience or disappoint you with their choices. Use this observational wealth in character creation. Instead of inventing personalities from scratch, draw from the patterns you've observed in real people. The way your mother-in-law deflects difficult conversations, your colleague's habit of taking credit for others' work, your neighbour's unexpected generosity during crises—these observed behaviours can become authentic character traits for fictional people in completely different circumstances.

Your family of origin provided you with a master class in human psychology and relationship dynamics. Even if you don't want to write directly about your family, you can use what you learned about how people function in intimate relationships to create believable fictional families. You understand how birth order affects personality, how family secrets shape behaviour, how people repeat or rebel against generational patterns, how love can coexist with frustration, how families develop their own languages and traditions. This knowledge allows you to create fictional families that feel real because they're based on deep understanding of how actual families work.

Your career experiences have exposed you to different types of people, organisational cultures, power dynamics, and social hierarchies. Whether you worked in corporate environments, helping professions, creative fields, or any other context, you've observed how people navigate authority, competition, collaboration and conflict. These observations can enrich fictional workplaces, social settings, and character interactions. You know how office politics actually work, how different personality types respond to authority, how people behave differently in public and private settings. This knowledge helps you create fictional worlds that feel authentic rather than idealised or oversimplified.

You've lived through significant historical and cultural changes, witnessing how society evolves and how people adapt to change. This firsthand experience of historical periods can add authentic detail to fiction set in eras you've lived through. You remember what it felt like when certain technologies were introduced, how social attitudes shifted over time, what daily life was like during different periods. This lived knowledge allows you to write period fiction with an authenticity that research alone can't provide.

The key to using life experience in fiction is transformation rather than transcription. Take the emotional core of an experience but change the external circumstances. Take the personality dynamics you've observed but place them in different settings. Take the themes that fascinate you but explore them through invented situations. This alchemy allows you to mine your experiences without being limited by them. You can explore 'what-if' scenarios: What if that difficult boss had been a parent instead of a supervisor? What if that family crisis had happened to strangers in a different culture? What if that moment of personal growth had occurred under completely different circumstances?

Finding Your Voice in Poetry: From Personal Expression to Universal Themes

Poetry offers unique opportunities for the writer to distil experience into its essence, to explore the emotional and spiritual dimensions of life, and to connect personal insight with universal human themes. Your accumulated experiences provide rich material for poetic exploration, while your emotional maturity allows you to approach poetry with depth and authenticity.

Most poets begin with what they know intimately—their own experiences, observations, and emotional responses. You have the advantage of a vast archive of experiences to draw from, as well as the perspective to understand which experiences contain universal resonance.

Begin with moments that still hold emotional charge for you: the death of a parent, the launch of a child into independence, a moment of unexpected beauty, a realisation about yourself or life, an encounter that shifted your perspective. These emotionally significant experiences often contain the seeds of powerful poems because they represent intersections between personal experience and larger human themes.

Universal themes are the fundamental experiences that characterise human existence across cultures, generations, and individual circumstances. Understanding these themes helps you recognise when your personal experiences connect to broader human concerns, making your poetry more widely relatable.

Core Universal Themes in Human Experience:

- Love and connection: romantic love, familial bonds, friendship, community, belonging, isolation, the search for understanding

- Loss and grief: death, separation, disappointment, the passage of time, change, letting go, mourning what never was

- Growth and transformation: coming of age, learning from mistakes, spiritual development, healing, forgiveness, personal evolution

- Identity and purpose: self-discovery, role changes, questioning meaning, finding direction, understanding one's place in the world

- Power and vulnerability: control vs surrender, strength and weakness, protecting others, being protected, independence vs dependence

- Time and mortality: ageing, legacy, regret, memory, the preciousness of moments, awareness of life's finite nature

- Justice and morality: right and wrong, fairness, responsibility, standing up for beliefs, moral complexity, ethical dilemmas

- Nature and transcendence: connection to the natural world, spiritual experiences, wonder, the search for meaning beyond the material

- Hope and despair: resilience, faith, doubt, finding light in darkness, endurance, the renewal of spirit.

Beyond Memoir

The art of poetry lies in presenting personal experience in ways that illuminate universal themes. This doesn't mean abandoning specificity—quite the opposite. The more specific and authentic your personal details, the more powerfully they can evoke universal experiences in readers.

For example, a poem about cleaning out your mother's house after her death might use specific details like her particular perfume still lingering in the closet and the handwritten grocery lists in her familiar handwriting to explore universal themes of grief, memory, and the physical presence of absence. The specific details make the universal experience tangible and emotionally accessible.

You can bring strengths to exploring universal themes. You've lived long enough to see patterns, to understand complexity, to appreciate paradox. You can write about love with knowledge of how it evolves over time. You can explore loss with understanding of how grief changes but doesn't end. You can examine hope with awareness of how it can coexist with realism.

This perspective allows for poetry that is both emotionally honest and philosophically sophisticated. You don't need to resolve contradictions or provide simple answers—you can explore the beautiful complexity of human experience.

Finding your poetic voice means discovering how you authentically speak about the things that matter to you. This often involves stripping away borrowed language, academic pretension, or attempts to sound 'poetic' in favour of your own genuine way of seeing and expressing. Mature writers often have an advantage here because they're less concerned with impressing others and more interested in authentic expression. You can focus on saying what you actually mean rather than what you think you should say.

Imaginative writing comes with both unique freedoms and particular challenges. Understanding both can help you make the most of this creative opportunity while navigating the obstacles that might discourage less experienced writers.

One of the greatest gifts is knowing yourself—your values, your voice, your particular way of seeing the world. This self-knowledge creates tremendous freedom in imaginative writing because you're no longer trying to figure out who you are while simultaneously trying to create art. You know what kinds of stories interest you, what themes resonate with your experience, what emotional territories you want to explore. You can write from conviction rather than experimentation, which often leads to more powerful, authentic work.

By now, you've likely faced significant challenges and survived them. This experience can provide courage for artistic risk-taking. You're less afraid of failure, criticism or rejection because you've learned that you can handle these setbacks and continue. This courage allows you to write about difficult topics, to explore controversial themes, to create characters who are flawed and complex, to tackle ambitious projects that might intimidate less experienced writers.

Writing Exercise

This exercise will help you explore how to transform your life experiences into fictional and poetic material while connecting personal insights to universal themes.

1: Experience Mining for Fiction

Think of five people you've known well who had distinctly different personalities. For each person, identify:

- One specific behaviour that revealed their character
- How they typically responded to stress or conflict
- What they valued most (even if they didn't state it directly)
- One surprising thing about them that others might not have noticed
- How they changed (or didn't change) over the time you knew them.

Now create a fictional character by combining elements from different people on your list. Give this character a name and place them in a situation completely different from any context where you knew the real people.

Choose a strong emotion you've experienced (grief, joy, anger, fear, love, betrayal, relief). Write about a fictional character experiencing this same emotion, but in completely different circumstances from your actual experience. Focus on the internal landscape—how the emotion feels physically, what thoughts it generates, how it affects the character's behaviour and perception.

2: Universal Theme Identification

List five to ten significant experiences from your life. For each experience, identify which universal themes it represents from this list:

- Love and connection
- Loss and grief
- Growth and transformation
- Identity and purpose
- Power and vulnerability
- Time and mortality
- Justice and morality
- Nature and transcendence
- Hope and despair.

Choose the theme that appears most frequently in your experiences or that feels most important to explore.

For your chosen universal theme, brainstorm:

- Different ways this theme might manifest in various people's lives
- Historical or cultural contexts where this theme would be particularly relevant
- Age groups or life stages where this theme might be most prominent
- Fictional scenarios that could explore this theme in fresh ways.

3: Poetry Voice Development

Choose one specific moment from your life that connects to your chosen universal theme. Write a poem about this moment using this structure:

- Stanza 1 (4–6 lines): set the specific scene with concrete, sensory details.
- Stanza 2 (4–6 lines): explore your emotional response to this moment.
- Stanza 3 (4–6 lines): connect this personal experience to the larger universal theme.
- Stanza 4 (4–6 lines): end with an insight, question or image that opens the experience to readers.

Don't worry about perfect rhyme or meter—focus on authentic expression and clear imagery.

Read your poem aloud. Does it sound like you speaking authentically about something that matters to you? Circle any words or phrases that feel borrowed from other poets or artificially 'poetic'. Consider replacing them with your own natural language.

4: Fiction Scenario Development

Take a significant relationship from your life (parent, spouse, child, friend, colleague) and transform it into fiction by changing:

- The setting (different time period, location, or cultural context)
- The external circumstances (different jobs, family situations, or life stages)
- The gender, age or background of one or both people
- The specific events while keeping the emotional dynamics.

Write a scene between these transformed characters that explores the same relationship dynamics you experienced, but in this new fictional context.

Review your scene. Does the emotional core feel authentic even though the external details are invented? Does the dialogue and behaviour ring true to human nature as you've observed it?

5: Creative Freedom Assessment

Complete these statements about your creative freedoms:

- Now that I know myself better, I feel free to write about …
- I'm no longer worried about what others think when I …
- My life experience gives me confidence to explore …
- I feel less need to prove myself and more desire to …
- The courage I've developed allows me to …

Complete these statements about creative challenges:

- I sometimes feel intimidated by …
- I need to learn more about …
- I get discouraged when I compare myself to …
- The time pressure I feel makes me …
- I could be more patient with myself when …

6: Genre Experimentation

Take the same emotional experience and try expressing it in three different forms:

- Write about what actually happened, focusing on factual accuracy and personal reflection.
- Transform the experience into a scene with invented characters in a different setting, focusing on emotional truth rather than factual accuracy.
- Distil the experience into imagery and emotion, focusing on the essence rather than the complete story.

o Which form felt most natural?

o Which allowed you to explore different aspects of the experience?

o Which felt most emotionally satisfying?

o Consider how different genres might serve different purposes in your writing life.

7: Development Planning

Based on this exploration, identify:

- Which genre (fiction, poetry, or both) most interests you for further development
- What technical skills you most need to develop

- How you might learn these skills (books, classes, workshops, online resources)
- What practice routine might help you develop in your chosen genre.

Sketch an idea for a longer project (short story collection, novel, poetry chapbook) that would allow you to explore your chosen universal theme through imaginative writing, drawing on your life experience for emotional authenticity while using fictional or poetic forms for creative freedom.

Remember: imaginative writing doesn't mean abandoning what you know—it means transforming what you know into new forms that can reach different audiences and explore different possibilities. Your life experience is not a limitation on your fiction and poetry; it's the foundation that makes your imaginative work authentic and emotionally resonant.

FINDING YOUR CREATIVE COMMUNITY

'I spent my first year of serious writing in complete isolation, thinking I needed to prove myself before I deserved to be around "real" writers. When I finally joined a local writing group for women over fifty, everything changed. Not only did I receive valuable feedback on my work, but I found my people, women who understood the unique challenges of starting a creative career at middle age, who celebrated small victories with genuine enthusiasm, and who reminded me that I wasn't crazy for wanting to write books at my age. That community became my lifeline, my cheering section, and my creative family.'

– Rose

Writing is often portrayed as a solitary pursuit, and while the actual act of putting words on paper happens alone, the creative life thrives in community. This is particularly true for women writers who may be navigating creative reinvention while managing complex life responsibilities. The right creative community provides encouragement during discouraging times, celebrates victories that others might not understand, offers practical advice about the writing life, and reminds you that you're not alone in this sometimes challenging but deeply rewarding journey.

Finding your creative community may require patience and intention. The perfect group for you might not exist yet, which means you might need to create it. Your ideal writing companions might be other writers who share your life stage and perspective, or they might be writers of all ages who share your passion for specific genres or approaches to craft. The key is finding people who support your creative growth while challenging you to develop your skills and vision.

Connecting with other writers who share your life stage offers unique benefits that mixed-age groups, while valuable, may not provide. These writers often face similar challenges: balancing creative work with caregiving responsibilities, overcoming internalised messages about age and creativity, managing the emotional complexity of writing about long-lived experiences, and navigating the publishing landscape as newcomers with established life expertise.

Midlife writers often bring similar perspectives to their creative work that can create immediate bonds and understanding. You're likely dealing with comparable life situations: adult children launching their own lives, ageing parents requiring more care, career transitions or retirement planning, health changes that affect energy and focus, and the existential questions that arise when you realise time is finite. This shared experience creates a foundation for deeper creative connection. When you share a draft about caring for a parent with dementia, other writers understand not just the craft elements but the emotional complexity you're navigating. When you discuss the challenge of finding time to write while managing multiple responsibilities, they offer practical solutions born from similar struggles.

Many writers struggle with similar internal obstacles: feeling like they're 'too late' to start a serious creative practice, comparing themselves to younger writers who seem more confident or technically advanced, or doubting whether their perspectives are relevant in contemporary literary culture. Being part of a community of writers helps normalise these concerns while providing living examples of people successfully overcoming them. Seeing other women your age completing manuscripts, getting published, or building writing careers provides concrete evidence that your creative dreams are achievable.

Writing communities combine decades of collective life experience with developing creative skills. This creates rich opportunities for learning that go beyond craft instruction. Group members often share professional expertise that supports each other's writing careers: one member might have marketing experience, another might have publishing connections, a third might have teaching skills that benefit the group. This peer-to-peer learning model often feels more comfortable than hierarchical teacher-student relationships, especially for accomplished professionals who are beginners only in writing.

Look for writing communities specifically designed for mature writers through:

- Local libraries and community centres that often host senior writing groups
- Community colleges that offer continuing education writing classes
- Organisations like AARP that sometimes sponsor creative programmes
- Online platforms like Meetup.com where you can search for age-specific writing groups
- Facebook groups dedicated to writers similar to you or that focus on specific genres (memoir writing for women over 50, second-career authors, etc.)
- Writing conferences and workshops that target mature audiences
- Retirement communities that often have active writing programmes.

If you can't find existing groups, consider that many other writers are looking for exactly what you're seeking. A simple email to friends, a post on social media, or a notice at your local library might connect you with others ready to form a new group.

Writing groups provide structure, accountability and community for your creative practice. Whether you join an existing group or start your own, the key is finding or creating a dynamic that supports everyone's growth while honouring different experience levels, writing goals, and personality types.

When evaluating potential writing groups, consider both the practical logistics and the group culture. Practical considerations include meeting frequency and location, group size, genre focus, and whether the group emphasises critique, support, or social connection. More importantly, assess the group culture during a visit or trial period. Does the feedback feel constructive rather than destructive? Do members celebrate each other's successes genuinely? Is there space for different types of writing and different definitions of success? Do you feel energised rather than drained after meetings? Pay attention to how the group handles conflict, manages different skill levels, and balances encouragement with honest feedback. A group that's too gentle may not help you grow, while one that's overly critical can damage confidence and creative risk-taking.

Creating your own writing group gives you control over the culture and focus but requires more initial investment of time and energy. Start by clarifying your vision: What kind of group do you want to create? What would make it valuable for you and others?

Consider these foundational decisions:

- Group size: 4 to 8 members usually works well for sustained conversation and adequate time for everyone.

- Meeting frequency: monthly meetings are often sustainable while weekly might be too demanding.
- Format: will you focus on critique, writing exercises, discussion, or a combination?
- Logistics: where will you meet? How long will meetings last? What materials or preparation are expected?
- Ground rules: how will you handle feedback, confidentiality, and group dynamics?

Successful writing groups usually establish clear guidelines about feedback, respect and participation. Consider adopting principles like:

- Feedback focuses on the writing, not the writer.
- Every piece shared receives some positive recognition along with suggestions for improvement.
- Members commit to regular attendance and participation.
- Confidentiality is maintained about shared work and personal information.
- Different writing goals and styles are respected.
- The group culture emphasises growth and encouragement over competition.

Online meeting platforms have expanded possibilities for writing group participation. Virtual groups allow you to connect with writers beyond your geographic area, can be easier to schedule around busy lives, and may feel less intimidating for shy participants. However, in-person groups often create stronger bonds and may be easier for less tech-savvy members. Many groups successfully combine both formats, meeting primarily in person with virtual backup options for weather or schedule conflicts.

Consider creative combinations of group activities: monthly critique meetings combined with quarterly social gatherings, writing retreats or workshop days, reading groups that discuss craft alongside published works, or accountability partnerships between meetings. Some groups find success with 'writing dates'—meeting primarily to write in each other's company with minimal discussion, providing company and gentle accountability without the pressure of sharing unfinished work.

Writing Exercise

This exercise will help you assess your current creative community, identify what type of support you need, and develop a practical plan for building the writing relationships that will sustain and inspire your creative work.

1: Current Community Assessment

Map your current sources of creative support and encouragement:

- Who in your life currently supports your writing goals?
- What friends or family members understand and encourage your creative work?
- Are there any writers in your current network, even casually?
- What online communities or groups do you currently participate in?
- Who provides feedback on your writing now, if anyone?

Identify what's missing from your current creative support system:

- Do you have people who understand the specific challenges of writing?
- Is there anyone who can provide knowledgeable feedback on your work?
- Do you have accountability for your writing goals and deadlines?
- Are there people who celebrate your writing victories with genuine enthusiasm?
- Do you have access to practical advice about the business side of writing?
- Is there anyone who challenges you to grow and take creative risks?

2: Community Needs Clarification

Describe your ideal writing community:

- What size group would feel most comfortable and productive for you?
- Do you prefer in-person, virtual or hybrid meeting formats?
- How often would you like to connect with your writing community?

- What balance do you want between social connection and focused work feedback?
- Do you want to focus on critique, encouragement, accountability or learning?
- What age range and experience level would feel most supportive?

From this list, identify your top three community needs:

- Regular feedback on work in progress
- Accountability for writing goals and deadlines
- Encouragement and emotional support for creative challenges
- Practical advice about publishing, marketing, or business aspects
- Social connection with people who understand creative work
- Learning opportunities to develop specific writing skills
- Collaboration opportunities for projects or events.

3: Writer Connection Strategy

Investigate community resources for connecting with other new writers:

- What libraries, community centres or colleges offer programmes for mature adults?
- Are there senior centres, retirement communities, or age-specific organisations with writing programmes?
- What bookstores, literary organisations, or cultural centres might host writing events?
- Do any local writing groups specifically welcome or target older writers?
- Are there memoir groups, life writing classes, or legacy projects in your area?

Research virtual opportunities for connecting with writers:

- What Facebook groups focus on writing or specific genres you're interested in?
- Are there online writing organisations that welcome mature members?
- What virtual conferences, workshops or events target older writers?
- Which online platforms (Meetup, Discord, specialised writing sites) might connect you with peers?
- Are there age-specific writing challenges, contests or programmes you could join?

4: Writing Group Options Assessment

Consider whether you'd prefer to join an existing group or start your own:

Joining existing groups – pros and cons:

- Less initial work and responsibility
- Established culture and practices
- May not perfectly match your needs or preferences
- Less control over group dynamics and direction.

Starting your own group – pros and cons:

- Complete control over culture, focus and logistics
- Can create exactly what you need
- Requires more initial investment of time and energy
- Responsibility for group success and maintenance.

Which approach feels more appealing and realistic for your current circumstances?

If you're leaning towards starting a group, begin planning the basics:

- How many members would you want initially?
- Where would you meet and how often?

- What would be your primary focus (critique, support, writing practice, etc.)?
- How would you find and invite initial members?
- What ground rules would be important to establish from the beginning?

5: Action Planning

Identify specific actions you'll take in the next month to build your creative community:

Week 1: Research and outreach

- What local and online communities will you research this week?
- Will you attend any writing events, visit groups, or join online communities?

Week 2: Initial connections

- How will you introduce yourself to potential community members?
- What groups will you visit or virtually attend?

Week 3: Evaluation and decision

- How will you assess which communities feel most promising?

- Will you commit to joining a group or start planning your own?

Week 4: Commitment and follow-through

- What specific commitment will you make to building creative community?
- How will you follow through on connections you've made?

Envision how you want your creative community to evolve over the next year:

- What role do you want community to play in your writing life?
- How will you maintain and nurture the relationships you build?
- What might you contribute to the broader writing community in your area or online?
- How will you know when you've found or created the creative community you need?

Remember: building creative community takes time and often requires trying several different groups or approaches before finding the right fit. Don't be discouraged if your first attempts don't immediately produce the connections you're seeking. The perfect writing community for you might not exist yet—which means you have the opportunity to help create it. Your willingness to reach out, participate and invest in creative relationships will not only benefit you but will help build the broader community that supports all writers in your area and stage of life.

THE ONGOING JOURNEY

> 'I started writing at fifty-two thinking I had one book in me—my memoir about caring for my mother with Alzheimer's. Seven years later, I've published three books, teach memoir workshops, and wake up every morning excited about the words waiting to be discovered. Writing didn't just give me a second career; it gave me a new relationship with time itself. Instead of feeling like life was winding down, I feel like I'm just getting started. Each day brings new observations, deeper insights, and fresh ways to understand the ongoing mystery of being human. At fifty-nine, I'm not the same writer I was at fifty-two, and I can't wait to see who I'll become as a writer at sixty-five, seventy, and beyond.'
>
> – Catherine

Writing is not a destination you arrive at but a journey that continues to unfold, deepen and transform throughout your life. The writer you are today is not the writer you'll be in five years, just as the person you are now has grown far beyond who you were when you first put pen to paper with serious intent. This ongoing evolution is one of the greatest gifts of a writing life—it ensures that your creative practice will continue to surprise, challenge and fulfil you for decades to come.

The journey ahead will include transitions you can anticipate and changes you cannot yet imagine. Your writing practice will need to adapt to shifting energy levels, evolving interests, changing life circumstances, and the inevitable losses and discoveries that come with continued living. The key is building a creative practice flexible enough to bend without breaking, rooted deeply enough to provide stability through whatever changes lie ahead.

The decades ahead will bring transitions both predictable and unexpected. Your writing practice can become a constant companion through these changes, sometimes providing comfort during difficult passages, sometimes capturing insights that emerge from new experiences, sometimes offering structure when other aspects of life feel uncertain. Some transitions are largely predictable: retirement from primary careers, the death of parents, changes in health and energy, shifts in living situations, evolving relationships with adult children, and the gradual letting go of roles that have defined earlier chapters of your life.

Each of these transitions brings both loss and opportunity. Retirement may mean the loss of professional identity but the gain of time and mental space for creative work. The death of parents brings grief but also a changed perspective on mortality, legacy, and what truly matters. Health changes may require adjustments to your writing practice but often deepen appreciation for the present moment and the preciousness of creative expression.

The Ongoing Journey

Your writing can serve multiple purposes during major transitions: processing the emotional complexity of change, preserving memories and insights before they fade, exploring new aspects of identity that emerge when old roles fall away, and maintaining continuity of self through periods of significant change. Life will also bring surprises—health crises, family emergencies, unexpected opportunities, global events that reshape daily life, or personal discoveries that change your understanding of yourself and your place in the world.

A flexible writing practice can adapt to unexpected circumstances while providing stability during turbulent times. When a health crisis limits your mobility, you might discover the intimacy of writing by hand. When family responsibilities temporarily consume your time, you might develop skill at capturing insights in brief moments. When unexpected opportunities arise, your writing background might open doors you never imagined.

The key is approaching your writing practice as a living system that can evolve and adapt rather than a rigid structure that might break under pressure.

As you continue to navigate life's transitions, your writing can serve as both witness and guide. Documenting your experiences creates a record of your journey through change—valuable not only for your own reflection but potentially helpful for others facing similar transitions. Your future writing might explore themes that feel distant now: what it means to age with dignity, how to find purpose in later decades, ways to maintain vitality and curiosity as energy shifts, or how to offer wisdom without becoming irrelevant. These explorations serve both personal processing and potential service to others walking similar paths.

Just as your writing practice might adapt to seasonal rhythms throughout the year, it can also adapt to the seasons of your life. The intense growth phase of early writing development might give way to periods of deeper exploration, followed by phases of sharing and teaching, and perhaps eventually periods of reflection and synthesis. Each phase brings different gifts and serves different purposes. The key is recognising and honouring where you are in your creative development while remaining open to continued growth and change.

The writer you are now represents just one point in your ongoing creative development. Your voice will continue to deepen, your skills will expand, your interests may shift, and your understanding of what you want to accomplish through writing will likely transform multiple times over the decades ahead.

Even if you've achieved competence in your preferred forms of writing, there's always more to learn. Your technical skills can continue improving, your artistic vision can expand, and your understanding of the craft can deepen throughout your writing life. You might discover new genres that intrigue you, develop expertise in areas that currently feel challenging, or find innovative ways to combine different forms of writing. The memoir writer might experiment with poetry, the fiction writer might try essays, or the blogger might develop a novel.

The Ongoing Journey

These explorations keep your creative practice fresh while expanding your capabilities.

Continuing education through workshops, conferences, reading and experimentation can provide ongoing stimulation for your creative development. Your decades of life experience combined with developing technical skill create unique opportunities for artistic growth that weren't available to you as a younger person.

Your authentic voice will continue to evolve as you do. The voice that emerges in your early writing represents your current understanding of yourself and your perspective on the world. As you continue living, learning, and gaining insight, your voice will naturally deepen and expand. This evolution might involve becoming more direct and confident in expressing your perspectives, developing greater nuance in exploring complex emotions, or finding new ways to connect personal experience with universal themes. Your voice might become more philosophical, more playful, more urgent, or more peaceful reflecting your own continued growth and change.

As your life continues to unfold, new experiences will provide fresh material for your writing. The themes that captivate you now could evolve, and entirely new areas of interest might emerge based on future experiences, relationships or discoveries. Your writing might explore ageing with curiosity rather than fear, examine what it means to be a wise elder in a rapidly changing world, or investigate questions about legacy, meaning and purpose that feel more urgent with each passing year. These future themes might feel abstract now but will likely become compelling as you live into them.

The tools and technologies available to writers continue to evolve rapidly. Your future writing practice might incorporate technologies that don't yet exist, distribution methods that haven't been invented, or forms of reader engagement that are still being developed. Staying open to technological innovation while maintaining focus on the essential elements of good writing, authentic voice, meaningful content, clear expression allows you to benefit from new opportunities without being overwhelmed by constant change.

Your growing experience and developing reputation as a writer may create opportunities for collaboration that aren't available to newer writers. You might co-author books with others who share your expertise, mentor younger writers in formal or informal capacities, or participate in anthologies or projects that bring together diverse voices around shared themes.

These collaborative opportunities can energise your creative practice while expanding your impact and connection with the broader writing community.

Perhaps the most important shift in perspective for writers is viewing writing not as a career phase or temporary pursuit but as a lifelong practice that will continue to enrich and be enriched by whatever lies ahead.

For many writers, the creative process becomes a form of spiritual practice; it is a way of connecting with something larger than themselves, processing the mystery of existence, and finding meaning in the ongoing experience of being human. This spiritual dimension of writing often deepens with age and experience. The questions that drive your writing might become more profound, your willingness to explore difficult topics more courageous, and your appreciation for the gift of expression more acute. Writing becomes not just what you do but part of who you are.

Your writing creates a legacy that extends far beyond published books or public recognition. Every word you write honestly contributes to the record of human experience. Your journals preserve insights and observations that might otherwise be lost. Your published work offers perspectives and wisdom to readers you may never meet. Even if your writing never reaches a large audience, it serves important purposes: processing your experiences, maintaining your intellectual vitality, preserving family and cultural history, and modelling creative engagement with life for those around you.

Research consistently shows that regular writing provides significant benefits for cognitive function, emotional processing, and overall well-being. These benefits become increasingly important with age, making your writing practice not just creative expression but also investment in your long-term health and vitality. The mental exercise of finding words for complex experiences, the emotional release of expressing difficult feelings, and the cognitive challenge of organising thoughts into coherent expression all contribute to maintaining sharp thinking and emotional resilience as you age.

Your commitment to creative expression now and beyond provides a powerful example for your children, grandchildren, peers, and community members that creativity and growth don't have expiration dates. You're helping to change cultural narratives about ageing and capability simply by continuing to create and share your work. This modelling function adds meaning to your writing practice beyond personal satisfaction. You're not just creating for yourself; you're demonstrating possibilities for others who might otherwise assume their creative opportunities have passed.

Writing Exercise

This final exercise will help you envision how your writing practice might evolve over the coming decades while creating concrete plans for sustaining and adapting your creative work through whatever changes lie ahead.

1: Future Transition Preparation

Consider the major life transitions you can reasonably anticipate over the next ten to twenty years:

- How might retirement or career changes affect your writing time and energy?
- What family transitions (aging parents, evolving relationships with adult children) might impact your creative focus?
- How could health changes or shifts in physical capability affect your writing practice?
- What living situation changes might require adaptation of your writing environment?
- How might your financial circumstances change in ways that affect your writing investments?

For each anticipated transition, consider:

- How could writing serve you during this change?
- What adaptations might your writing practice require?
- What opportunities for new material or perspectives might emerge?
- How could you prepare now to maintain creative continuity through these transitions?

Identify elements of your writing practice that could provide stability during uncertain times:

- What aspects of your creative routine are least dependent on external circumstances?
- How could you develop multiple ways to engage with writing (different tools, locations, formats)?
- What support systems could help maintain your creative practice during difficult periods?
- How might you build flexibility into your writing goals and expectations?

2: Creative Evolution Visioning

Envision how your writing abilities might develop over time:

- What aspects of craft do you most want to improve over the next 5 to 10 years?
- What new genres or forms might you explore as your confidence grows?
- How might your unique voice continue to develop and deepen?
- What themes or subjects might become more important to you as you gain more life experience?
- How could your growing expertise create opportunities for teaching, mentoring or collaboration?

Consider how your perspectives and priorities might shift:

- What questions or themes might become more important to you as you age?
- How might your relationship with success, achievement and recognition evolve?
- What wisdom or insights might you develop that could inform your future writing?
- How could your growing understanding of mortality affect your creative priorities?
- What legacy do you want to create through your continued writing?

3: Lifelong Practice Design

Envision writing as a constant presence throughout your remaining years:

- How might writing serve different purposes at different life stages?
- What would it mean to approach writing as a spiritual practice or ongoing exploration?
- How could your writing practice provide continuity through major life changes?
- What would it look like to write primarily for the joy and growth it provides rather than external outcomes?

Plan for how your practice might adapt to changing circumstances:

- How could you maintain creative engagement if physical limitations affect your current writing methods?
- What alternative forms of creative expression might complement or substitute for traditional writing?
- How might you involve others (family, collaborators, communities) in supporting your continued creative practice?
- What technologies or tools might expand your creative possibilities as they develop?

4: Legacy and Impact Visioning

Consider the lasting impact of your writing life:

- What do you hope your writing will mean to your family in future generations?
- How might your creative practice influence others in your community?
- What contributions do you want to make to the broader conversation about ageing, creativity, or your areas of expertise?
- How does your writing serve purposes beyond personal expression?

Envision your role in the broader writing community:

- How might you support other writers as you gain experience and confidence?
- What knowledge or perspectives could you share through teaching or mentoring?
- How could you contribute to changing cultural narratives about age and creativity?
- What communities might you help build or strengthen through your continued writing?

5: Practical Sustainability Planning

Plan for the practical aspects of sustaining a lifelong writing practice:

- How will you continue funding your writing activities (education, books, conferences, professional services)?
- What support systems will help you maintain motivation and accountability over time?
- How might you balance writing with other interests and responsibilities as they evolve?
- What health and wellness practices will support your long-term creative vitality?

Create a framework for ongoing goal setting that can adapt to changing circumstances:

- What core values will guide your writing decisions regardless of external changes?
- How will you balance ambitious long-term projects with flexible short-term goals?
- What measures of success will remain meaningful to you throughout your writing life?
- How will you maintain creative curiosity and openness to new possibilities?

The Ongoing Journey

6: Commitment and Intention Setting

Write a personal manifesto for your lifelong writing practice:

- I commit to continuing my writing practice because …
- Through the transitions and changes ahead, writing will serve me by …
- I will adapt my practice as needed while maintaining …
- My writing will contribute to the world by …
- I trust that my creative journey will continue to …

Identify specific actions you'll take in the next month to support your long-term writing vision:

- What will you do to prepare for anticipated transitions?
- How will you begin developing skills or exploring areas you want to grow into?
- What relationships or communities will you cultivate to support your continued development?
- How will you celebrate and acknowledge your writing journey so far?

Take a moment to appreciate the courage it took to begin this writing journey and the wisdom you've already gained along the way. Your commitment to creative expression represents not just personal growth but a gift to everyone who witnesses your example. The words you write, the stories you tell, and the persistence you demonstrate in pursuing your creative dreams contribute to a more expansive understanding of what's possible at every stage of life.

Your writing journey is just beginning. The best words, the deepest insights, and the most meaningful connections with readers may still lie ahead. Trust the process, embrace the ongoing adventure, and remember that every word you write honestly adds something valuable to the world.

Welcome to your lifelong practice. Welcome to the ongoing journey. Welcome to the rest of your writing life.

ABOUT THE AUTHOR

Vanessa McKay is an author, editor, publisher, coach and creative writing instructor based in Kwinana, Western Australia. Her journey as a writer began in childhood, fuelled by a deep-seated need to make sense of her world and find her voice. Through years of perseverance, self-discovery and honing her craft, Vanessa has emerged as a contemporary fiction author with four published novels and more to come.

Drawing from her rich life experiences and the challenges she's overcome, Vanessa now dedicates herself to nurturing other writers' creative spirits. She conducts engaging workshops, creating supportive environments where aspiring authors can explore their potential and develop their unique voices.

Vanessa's teaching philosophy emphasises the importance of a regular writing practice, embracing one's authentic self, and the power of persistence in the face of self-doubt. In addition to her local and online classes, Vanessa hosts immersive creative writing retreats, offering writers the opportunity to deeply engage with their craft in inspiring settings. These retreats combine focused writing time with guided exercises, group discussions and one-on-one mentoring sessions.

With a warm, encouraging approach and a wealth of personal insights, Vanessa is dedicated to empowering writers at all stages of their journey, helping them to unlock their creativity and share their stories with the world.

REFERENCES

M Al-Khouja, N Weinstein, W Ryan, N Legate (2022), 'Self-Expression Can Be Authentic or Inauthentic, with Differential Outcomes for Well-Being: Development of the Authentic and Inauthentic Expression Scale (AIES)', Journal of Research in Personality, Volume 97, 104191, ISSN 0092-6566, https://doi.org/10.1016/j.jrp.2022.104191.

F Callard, DS Margulies (2014), 'What We Talk About When We Talk About the Default Mode Network', Frontiers in Human Neuroscience, Aug 25, 8:619, doi: 10.3389/fnhum.2014.00619.

R Khalil, B Godde, AA Karim (2019), 'The Link Between Creativity, Cognition, and Creative Drives and Underlying Neural Mechanisms', Front Neural Circuits, Mar 22, 13:18, doi: 10.3389/fncir.2019.00018.

A Perera (2024), 'Fluid Intelligence vs. Crystallized Intelligence', https://www.simplypsychology.org/fluid-crystallized-intelligence.html.

www.ingramcontent.com/pod-product-compliance
Lightning Source LLC
LaVergne TN
LVHW051216070526
838200LV00063B/4918